T0160910

TELL IT TO THE WORLD

Stan Grant is an award-winning journalist and author. He is currently the global affairs and indigenous affairs analyst at the Australian Broadcasting Corporation. Prior to this, he worked as the indigenous editor for *The Guardian* Australia, managing editor for National Indigenous Television, and international editor for Sky News Australia. From 2001 to 2012, he served as a senior international correspondent for CNN in Asia and the Middle East, broadcasting to an audience of millions around the world. Stan is of Aboriginal ancestry, from the Wiradjuri people.

ALSO BY STAN GRANT

The Tears of Strangers

TELL IT TO THE
WORLD

STAN GRANT

SCRIBE

Melbourne • London

Scribe Publications
18–20 Edward St, Brunswick, Victoria 3056, Australia
2 John St, Clerkenwell, London, WC1N 2ES, United Kingdom
3754 Pleasant Ave, Suite 100, Minneapolis, Minnesota 55409 USA

First published as *Talking to My Country* in 2016 by HarperCollins*Publishers*
Australia Pty Limited
Published as *Talking to My Country* by Scribe in the UK 2016
Published by Scribe in North America 2019

Lines from 'Theme for English B' (Hughes) © reproduced with kind
permission by Harold Ober Associates Incorporated.
Lyrics from *She Cried*, written by Frank Yamma (*Mushroom Music Publishing*),
reproduced with kind permission.
Lyrics from *Took the Children Away*, written by Archie Roach (*Mushroom Music
Publishing*), reproduced with kind permission.

Typeset in Minion Pro Regular by Kirby Jones
Printed and bound in the UK by CPI Group (UK) Ltd, Croydon CR0 4YY

Scribe Publications is committed to the sustainable use of natural resources and
the use of paper products made responsibly from those resources.

9781947534261 (US edition)
9781925938005 (e-book)

scribepublications.com

To my grandmother Ivy and my wife Tracey –

white women who have loved us.

So will my page be Colored that I write?

Being me, it will not be white.

But it will be

a part of you …

You are white –

yet a part of me, as I am a part of you …

Sometimes, perhaps you don't want to be a part of me.

Nor do I often want to be a part of you.

But we are, that's true!

Langston Hughes: 'Theme For English B'

Contents

Introduction

I was about thirteen years old when I discovered James Baldwin. I stumbled upon his novel *Go Tell It on the Mountain*.

It was the title that drew me in. I had always loved the song "Go Tell It on the Mountain". Like Baldwin, I had a lot of religion in me. Old-time religion. Like Baldwin, I had been raised in the church — the black church.

This was the church of fire and brimstone. This was the church of sin and redemption. We worshipped the sacrificial Jesus of the cross. Matthew 27:46: "*Eloi, Eloi, lama sabachthani?*" — "My God, my God, why hast thou forsaken me?"

For we were the forsaken. Ours was the King James Bible — not for us any standardized version. We wanted the sound of the word of God. We loved how the old words rolled around our tongues.

My mother would spit my hair down and put me in my best shorts and shirt each Sunday to go to the mission church. My uncle — my father's brother — was the pastor. It was an exalted position in our community. Drunks would stand up straighter when he walked by, and mothers would silence their kids.

My uncle played his role with aplomb. I can still hear him thundering from the pulpit, a handkerchief mopping the sweat from his brow as he pointed at the congregation. We knew he was talking to us.

Luke 17:2: "It were better for him that a millstone were hanged about his neck, and he cast into the sea, than that he should offend one of these little ones."

His words hung as heavy as the air, my nausea rising with the heat, my neck stiffening as my temples throbbed. It was all I could do not to flee the church. I knew outside the air was sweet with fruit from the orchards that bordered the mission.

The fast-running currents of the irrigation channel promised relief from the swelter. The channel was a foreboding place. It had taken the lives of so many of our people who had fallen in, drunk. The channel was guarded by a blanket of sharp-edged burrs — catheads, we called them — jagged, vicious things that, once piercing the skin, would burn for hours.

Cooped in that little wooden church with my uncle's shout and spit, I would risk it all to run. But of course I couldn't escape my mother's eye — she would cast me sideways disapproving glances when she sensed my irritation growing.

The hymns we sung were old and forlorn. "The Old Rugged Cross", "Amazing Grace", "Shall We Gather at the River":

Soon we'll reach the silver river,
Soon our pilgrimage will cease,
Soon our happy hearts will quiver
With the melody of peace.

All of these songs promised a better day — because a better day was all we could hope for.

These days of sermon and song prepared me for James Baldwin. *Go Tell It on the Mountain* was the story he had to tell. It was his life in the church. It was his life among his people. Here was the story of two brothers, John and Roy, their father, the preacher — histories hidden, bodies buried, and children left to untangle a family's secrets.

This was the world slavery made. It came out of the black American experience, but it spoke powerfully to me, a boy from another world and time.

I was an Australian Aboriginal boy living in a family that had been banished from their country; like so many Aboriginal families — black families — we had been excluded and segregated. We were outcasts, existing on the margins of small towns in the Australian outback.

That's why Baldwin spoke to me: he reached across worlds to make sense of mine. I was in love with books and words, hungry for ideas. Baldwin sounded like home. We were living in a world that could not see us, and Baldwin made me visible.

Before Baldwin, books were entertainment. I spent many hours with Mark Twain, Robert Louis Stevenson, Charles Dickens, Arthur Conan Doyle. My mother would scrounge books wherever she could. I don't recall much in the way of birthday or Christmas presents — a scooter and a bike stand out — but I devoured my most treasured gift, a book of Greek myths.

I was transported to the world of Icarus and Narcissus and Zeus.

But Baldwin fixed me in the firmament — the place between worlds separating the waters of the white and the waters of the black. Here was a place for me. Here was a writer of courage and truth. The people of his book arrived fully formed; they didn't exist as a reflection of whiteness, this wasn't blackness as imagined, but real and flawed and courageous and pitiful. These were people who surprised and disappointed. These were people — black people — who were human.

Baldwin said, "I wish only to be an honest man and a good writer."

He was both. A black man confronting his country's legacy of racism. A son confronting his father's hypocrisy. A gay man confronting his sexuality. He became a touchstone for me.

After *Go Tell It on the Mountain*, I devoured whatever I could find. Baldwin's essays were searing meditations on race and history, each line quotable and a lesson in life. Words so brutally rendered that they make me wince even now. Words now unutterable and almost unthinkable.

"For the state, a nigger is a nigger is a nigger … sometimes Mr or Mrs or Dr Nigger."

They speak to the America of Black Lives Matter, the America that has questioned the citizenship of the first black president, as powerfully as they spoke to the Jim Crow–segregated south.

In *Nobody Knows My Name*, he wrote: "I have spent most of my life … watching white people and outwitting them so that I might survive."

By the time I read that, I had already figured out that dance for myself. How to navigate a world where I was always underestimated, trapped by the tyranny of low expectations.

But Baldwin gave voice to what I knew but could not say.

On the centenary of the emancipation proclamation — the freeing of the slaves — Baldwin wrote *The Fire Next*

Time, a letter to his nephew, his brother's son: "I know what the world has done to my brother", he wrote, "and how narrowly he has survived it. And I know, which is much worse, and this is the crime of which I accused my country and countrymen and for which neither I nor time nor history will ever forgive them, that they have destroyed and are destroying hundreds of thousands of lives and do not know it and do not want to know it."

I have returned so often to Baldwin in recent years. I have read again his words and felt their pull. They have spoken as powerfully to me today as they did when first I read them.

What a world they reveal. The tragedy of so many lives laid waste. I turned to Baldwin when I heard the news that another indigenous child had taken her life. She was only ten years old, living in a remote north-western corner of Western Australia.

Ten years old — we know what that looks like, what that should look like. Ten years old should be giggling at the back of the school bus. Ten years old should be swapping notes behind the teacher's back in class. Ten years old should be singing into a hairbrush and dancing in front of a mirror.

But ten years old to this girl looked like hopelessness.

This would be shocking if it were rare … but for Australia's first peoples this is so numbingly familiar.

Indigenous kids under the age of fourteen are almost ten times more likely to kill themselves than other Australians.

I turned again to Baldwin, when I saw images on my television of Aboriginal boys locked up and abused. They were being held in one of the most notorious juvenile-detention centers in Australia. One of them was filmed strapped to a chair, his head bound in a hood. It looked more like something from Iraq's Abu Ghraib prison than anything in my own country. I was reminded that, in Australia, Aboriginal people are fewer than 3 per cent of the population, yet make up a quarter of those in prisons and half of children detained.

I needed Baldwin to make sense of this. James Baldwin — so unflinching, so unbowed a man, writing free of the white gaze.

I turned again to the letter to his nephew, *The Fire Next Time*: "You were born into a society which spelled out with brutal clarity, and in as many ways as possible, that you were a worthless human being."

Is this too harsh? Are we too still deemed worthless?

My instinct is to soften the blow. Even knowing what I know, I struggle to accept that this is my country, that this is still who we are. I think of my fellow Australians of goodwill — those who have loved and cried with us — and I say surely this is the true measure of us.

But then I think again how 97 per cent of kids locked

up in the Northern Territory of Australia are black kids. I think of their parents too likely to have been behind bars. I think of their grandparents likely gone too soon … dead before their time. In this country, indigenous people die ten years younger than other Australians.

I think of how suicide remains the single biggest cause of death for indigenous people under the age of thirty-five. I think of Aboriginal women forty-five times more likely to suffer domestic violence than their white sisters. An Aboriginal woman is more than ten times more likely to be killed from violent assault. I think of lives chained to generations of misery.

To write of this is to cast aside doubt. It is to care more for what is said than what will be read — to be concerned less with how the reader may feel than to honor those whose lives I write about. To write of this is to write free of the white gaze.

The white gaze — it is a phrase that resonates in Black American literature. Writers from W.E.B. Du Bois to Ralph Ellison to Baldwin and Toni Morrison have struggled with it and railed against it.

As Morrison, a Nobel Laureate, once said: "Our lives have no meaning, no depth without the white gaze. And I have spent my entire writing life trying to make sure that the white gaze was not the dominant one in any of my books."

The white gaze: it traps black people in white imaginations. It is the eyes of a white schoolteacher who sees a black student and lowers expectations. It is the eyes of a white cop who sees a black person and looks twice — or, worse, feels for a gun.

Du Bois explored this more than a century ago in his book *The Souls of Black Folk*, reflecting on his conversations with white people and the ensuing delicate dance around the "Negro problem".

"Between me and the other world there is an ever unasked question … All, nevertheless, flutter around it … Instead of saying directly, how does it feel to be a problem? They say, I know an excellent colored man in my town … To the real question … I answer seldom a word."

The flame has passed to a new generation.

Over the past few years I have looked to three more black writers who have stared down the white gaze. In their own ways, Ta-Nehisi Coates, Claudia Rankine, and George Yancy have held up a mirror to white America. These are uncompromising and fearless voices.

Coates' searing essay *Between the World and Me* critiques America against a backdrop of black deaths at the hands of police. He says the country's history is rooted in slavery and the assault against the black body.

In the form of a letter to his son, Coates writes: "Here is what I would like for you to know: In America it is traditional to destroy the black body — it is heritage."

In *Citizen: an American lyric*, poet Claudia Rankine reflects on the black experience from the victims of Hurricane Katrina, or Trayvon Martin, a seventeen-year-old black youth shot dead by a Neighborhood Watch volunteer who was acquitted, or black tennis star Serena Williams. In each case, Rankine sees lives framed by whiteness.

She writes: "Because white men can't police their imagination, black men are dying."

Philosophy professor George Yancy penned a letter in *The New York Times* addressed to "Dear White America". He asks his countrymen to listen with love, and to look at those things that might cause pain and terror. All white people, he says, benefit from racism, and this means that each, in their own way, are racist: "Don't run to seek shelter from your own racism … practice being vulnerable. Being neither a 'good' white person nor a liberal white person will get you off the proverbial hook."

Their unflinching work is not tempered by the fact a black man was in the White House — that only makes their voices more urgent.

Coates, Rankine, Yancy — each has been variously praised and awarded, yet each has been pilloried as well. This is inevitable when some people don't like what the mirror reflects. It takes courage for a black person to speak to a white world, a world that can render invisible people of color, unless they begin to more closely resemble white people themselves — with an education, a house in the suburbs, a good job, lighter skin.

In Australia, too, black voices are defying the white gaze. We may not have the popular cut-through of a Morrison or a Baldwin or a Coates, but we have a proud tradition of Aboriginal writers, all with their own styles and genres, but together a united voice of defiance and survival.

This is a world so instantly recognizable to us — the First Peoples of our land — but a world still so foreign to white Australia.

I think of Natalie Harkin's book of poetry, *Dirty Words*, a subversive dictionary that turns English words back on their users: A is apology, B is for Boat People ... G is for Genocide ... S for Survival.

"How do you dream," she writes, "When your lucky country does not sleep?".

Bruce Pascoe's award-winning *Dark Emu* challenges the white stereotype of the "primitive hunter gatherer". He reveals a thriving pre-contact economy and culture. His voice challenges the very foundation of modern Australia. He repudiates the myth of terra nullius — this was not an empty land, there were people here with law and civilization. Britain chose not to see it.

That these works are not more widely read in Australia is a national shame, but I hope they can be read more widely here and across the world. George Yancy asks white Americans to become "un-sutured", to open themselves up and let go of their white innocence.

Why is this important? Well, for white people it may simply be a matter of choice — the fate of black people may not affect them. For us, it is survival — the white gaze means we die young, are locked up, and locked out of work and education.

When I came to write this book, I came with Baldwin as my guide. I came to write free of the white gaze, yet aware too that to understand myself, to understand my country, was to understand how we are reflected in our country's whiteness.

I am born of deep traditions. My footprints trace the first steps on this land. Yet I am born, too, of the white imagination — this imagination that said we did not exist. The imagination that said this was an empty land.

It is not just a legal doctrine; it is a state of mind. We were rendered invisible, our rights extinguished. If we existed at all, if we were visible at all, it was as the fly-blown savages unfit to be counted among the civilized races of the earth. Our story here was a story written in other lands — colonization, subjugation, brutal dispossession.

As Canadian political scientist Joyce Green has written:

"The dehumanization of Indigenous peoples was necessary for dispossession and subsequent judicial oppression."

Dispossession and oppression — the white gaze that justified or could turn a blind eye to the ravages of massacre and disease that devastated my people.

It was the white gaze that left no place for us in this new nation. It was the white gaze that at the time of federation forecast our doom — a race bound for extinction and not fit to be counted among the citizens of this country.

We hear the white gaze in the words of Australia's second prime minister, Alfred Deakin, who described Aboriginal people as a "dying race".

By the time I was born in 1963, the white gaze had placed us on the fringes of society — on the outside looking in. My parents' lives had been signed by the fires of bigotry and poverty. We moved from town to town, my father having little to offer but his muscle and his willingness to work.

I wonder now when I hear the sneering judgment of some in our own media mocking Aboriginal parents — lecturing them on their failure of responsibility, claiming that they are to blame for their children being beaten and locked up —where is the kind word and praise for people like my parents? And they were just two of the many Aboriginal mothers and fathers who have held their families together against overwhelming odds.

I value freedom of expression because it leaves us

nowhere to hide; it reveals people for who they are. Of course we have our failings, and some parents fall short in this. We are little different than others. But why do some take so much joy in pointing out the faults of indigenous people? Why revel in hurting those who already suffer the most?

I wonder if these people smug in their place in Australia would have looked upon me as a child — a dozen schools before I was in my teens, no permanent home, an itinerant laborer father, a gypsy caravan of extended family, born black and poor — and argued that I would have been better removed from those who loved me?

Yet this same family raised me from sawmill shacks to a career as an international journalist. I have had a front-row seat to history, reporting war in Iraq and Afghanistan, terrorism, revolution, and natural disaster. I have stood in the Great Hall of the People in Beijing and the Oval Office of the White House.

My journey has taken me around the world. I have spent much of my professional life reporting on countries and peoples who could not hold, torn apart by age-old enmities: religion, history, ideology.

I have witnessed first-hand the troubles of Northern Ireland that pitted Catholic against Protestant; the cold war relic of North Korea; the nuclear faultline of Kashmir, and the existential stand-off between Pakistan and India;

the rise of China and its mantra of throwing off a hundred years of foreign humiliation; and the bloodied borders of the Middle East.

I found a personal liberation in these countries torn by their own histories, yet where I could walk free of mine.

The philosopher Soren Kierkegaard said: "Life can only be understood backwards, but it must be lived forwards."

I returned after many years to my country to walk in my past, in order to find a way forward; to pierce what anthropologist Bill Stanner once called "the great Australian Silence".

I am of my people — the first people of this land — yet I have lived far from them. I have made a life in an Australia that still denies the rights of my people, and I can never truly find peace here.

I am a writer, and writers cannot belong. I live in the world of words and stories. I come from a long line of storytellers — I look to the world of poets, not politics. Poetry is the world of truth, and politics the world of the possible.

As always for me, there is James Baldwin. He wrote against the hopelessness of racism and its unspeakable crimes. He entered a world of spiritual darkness, to shine a path for those like me to follow.

He gave me a way to feel free. Ultimately, he gave me the greatest touchstone of all: myself.

My country: Australia

These are the things I want to say to you. These things I have held inside or even worse run from. It is not easy, what I have to say, and it should not be easy. These are things that tear at who we are. These are the things that kill, that spread disease and madness. These are the things that drive people to suicide, that put us in prisons and steal our sight.

I have started this so many times and stopped. I have tried to find the right words. It is so tempting to turn to rage and blame. I am angry: I know that. It flares suddenly and with the slightest provocation; it takes my breath away sometimes. I know where that comes from. I have seen it in my father and he inherited it from his father. It comes from the weight of history.

I am afraid too. And that comes from the same place. I have known this fear all my life. When I was young it used to make me feel sick, physically ill in the pit of my stomach. It was a fear of what could touch us – the sense of powerlessness, of being at the mercy of the intrusion of the police or the welfare officers who enforced laws that enshrined our exclusion and condemned us to poverty. It was a heavy hand that made people tremble. I see it still in my father. I see it as he tenses up just at the sight of a police car. He has done nothing wrong. But when he is pulled over for something as routine as a random breath test his heart beats faster and he fumbles his keys. We fear the state and we have every reason to. The state was designed to scare us.

I want to tell you about blood and bone and how mine is buried deep in this land. I want to tell you of a name that should be mine, a Wiradjuri name that passed down from thousands of years of kinship – taken from us along with our language and our land. And I want to tell you how I came to the name I have: Grant, the name of an Irishman, a name from a time of theft and death.

Australia still can't decide whether we were settled or invaded. We have no doubt. Our people died defending their land and they had no doubt. The result though was the same for us whatever you call it. Within a generation the civilisations of the eastern seaboard – older than the Pharaohs – were ravaged.

Across Australia nations that had not seen a white man – Bandjalang, Kamilaroi, Ngarrindjeri, Arabana, Darumbal, Gurindji, Yawuru, Watjarri, Barkindji, and all of the other hundreds of distinct peoples, each with their law and song and dance, all of them separate with their own boundaries defined by kinship and trade – in the eyes of the British simply never existed.

Soon we would lose our names; names unique, inherited from our forefathers. Then our languages silenced. Soon children would be gone. This is how we disappear. Now Australians pay their respects to the elders of nations of which they have no idea.

I want to tell you how you have always sought to define us. You called us Aborigines: a word that meant nothing to my people. And in that one word you erased our true identities. Today we have to prove constantly who we are. Australia's own government records show how we have been defined and redefined sixty-seven times: sixty-seven versions of us. We were classified according to a so-called 'quantum of blood', 'Full Blood', 'Half Caste', 'Quarter Caste', 'Octoroon'. Some were deemed to be Aborigines if they lived on a government mission or reserve; others were reclassified 'white' if they lived in town. Some people were granted a special status – exempted from restrictive or discriminatory laws. Today there is a three-part definition: indigenous descent, indigenous identity and acknowledgment by the indigenous community.

Whenever we enrol in school, apply for a job or join a sports team there is a box to tick that asks if we are Aboriginal or Islander. No one else is asked this. If we tick yes we have to prove it. My children have to ask their grandfather – a member of the Wiradjuri Council of Elders – to verify the identity of his own flesh and blood.

I was raised to know I was the son of a Wiradjuri man and a Kamilaroi woman – this is my family, my heritage – yet in the eyes of the state my identity remains in flux. To proclaim myself an indigenous person is a political act, something to be negotiated between our bloodline and the law imposed on us.

So, my country, these things are important. Faces and names and language and land are important. Without land we have no inheritance. People with no land are poor. It isn't just here: we share this with indigenous people throughout the world. Together we are just five per cent of the global population and fifteen per cent of total poverty. But these are numbers, and faces and names are far too often forgotten.

Australians know so little about us. They know so little about what has happened here in their name. Perhaps they can talk about the American west: Sitting Bull and Custer and Little Big Horn. They may know of Caesar and Napoleon and Tutankhamen. But Pemulwuy? Windradyne? Jandamurra? What of these warriors and leaders who fought and died here for their land? What about the massacres of Myall Creek, Coniston or Risdon Cove?

I have always thought settler communities unique, they see new lands as something to be claimed, as places without a past. The people who have come here have left history behind. Settlers look out; they look forward. The mark of success is to leave a better life for your children. Settlers prove how much they belong by how far they have travelled, how much they have acquired.

Because history is ignored, though, because the darkness of our past often goes unspoken, does not mean it doesn't plague us.

My country, I have hesitated to tell you of these things before. I have never been convinced you have wanted to hear. There are those now who will shrug. Others may pause and move on. But something else is moving in our country. We are looking again at reckoning with ourselves. I can feel it and many of you have told me you are ready.

In the winter of 2015 we turned to face ourselves. It happened in that place most sacred to us: the sporting field. Adam Goodes an indigenous footballer, one of the greatest players of his generation, was abused and humiliated until he could take it no more.

As this man retreated from the field we were forced to confront the darkest parts of this country – black and white we are all formed by it. This wasn't about sport; this was about our shared history and our failure to reconcile it. Some sought to deny this, others to excuse it, but when thousands of voices booed Adam Goodes, my people knew where that came from.

So here we are: all of us in this country – our country. Tethered to each other – black and white, the sons and daughters of settlers, the more recent migrants and my people with tens of thousands of years of tradition. I have to accept you because we are so few and have no choice. And anyway, you are in me and I am part of you. You can turn away from our plight, but while you do your anthem will forever ring hollow. And I don't believe that is who you are.

The truth for me is that I love Australia and I must love its people. I have dear friends who are white and I love them. And I love the mother of my son. I love more easily than I can forgive. So we must learn who we are, and see ourselves as if for the first time.

All of this is our story. These are events and faces and memories all set against the drama of this land. Our lives are pages of a history still unwritten, a story of a place and its people; the sins and triumphs and how all of it has formed us.

The great American playwright Eugene O'Neill said: 'There is no present or future, only the past happening over and over again.' The past is alive in me now. Its wounds rest deep and uneasily in our soul. I am the sum of many things but I am all history. And we are trapped in this history, all of us, and if we don't understand it we will remain chained to it. I am the product of a name – Grant – and genes and story but above it all I am what you have made me.

My country: Australia.

PART ONE

I want to tell you about the road that leads to my parents' house. It was here my people were murdered.

Today it is marked with a sign that reads: Poison Waterholes Creek. I could not count the number of times I have passed by here. Now I have brought my youngest son to sit by the cool water, under the shade of the trees. It is time he learned the truth of our history.

He is of an age now when he would become a man in the law of our ancestors. He would be put through the burbung – a secret and sacred ceremony to have the markings of manhood carved on his body. Now I am initiating him into the story of this land.

I was raised here: this place is alive to me. I have been gone for so long, but it still envelops me. The effect it has on me is physical. When I am home I breathe more deeply. I sleep long and still. I wake to the morning more slowly.

I like nothing more than to stand alone outside and feel the soft warm breeze on my skin. My eyes rest on detail that I am blind to in the city where I now live. I like the way an old nail protrudes from a wooden plank in my parents' shed. I like the way the corrugated iron roof – rusted and worn – bends at the corners. This is how a place bends over time. I like that spot where the dirt laneway meets the grass. I like the crunch of gravel under my feet. These things – little things – remind me that we live here; that we have shaped this place to fit us.

This country has shaped us too. It breathes in and out folding us into the empty spaces, each generation becoming part of the land itself. We are buried here, gravestones marking our resting places. We count the years in life and loss and our attachment grows deeper and stronger.

My people have been here forever. If I travel just a few hours I will come to a place where we fished, danced, sang, celebrated life and buried our dead with great ceremony. There was once a mighty lake here. Now it is dry with waves of sand frozen in place and craters like the surface of the moon.

On 26 February 1974 a rainstorm lashed the lake. It was just enough to loosen the hard packed soil. Jim Bowler, a young geologist, spotted a skull poking just above the surface. He cleared the loose sand and what he found altered our entire view of life on this continent. Lying there was an intact skeleton, buried in this ground for 40,000 years. It wasn't his first discovery. Years earlier Bowler had uncovered the remains of a female. Together they are known as Mungo Man and Woman, named after the lake where they lived.

These findings doubled the known length of time my people had lived in this land. They are the oldest human remains ever found in Australia. Mungo Man had been a hunter. His body ached with arthritis. His elbow was chipped and worn. He had died when he was around fifty years old. But what happened next was truly extraordinary. He was placed in a grave on his back, his arms folded across his body. He was smeared with red ochre. Mungo Woman had been cremated. These were funerals, the oldest evidence of such ritual anywhere on earth.

They lived during what scientists call the Pleistocene Age. It was a time of great glaciers, when up to a third of the world's surface was covered in ice. The runoff from the glaciers formed large lakes. At the other extreme deserts were drier and larger than they are now.

Enormous creatures roamed the land. There were mammoths, a species of woolly rhinoceros, sabre tooth cats, in Australia a huge wombat-shaped animal called a diprotodon and a giant goanna. The land was different; a person could walk from the tip of what is now New Guinea to the southern coast of Tasmania.

It was in this time that people spread throughout the continents. Homo sapiens – modern humans – evolved on the plains of Africa and emerged to dominate the planet. The people who would give birth to the great religions, form huge armies, wage brutal war, write great symphonies and plays, and walk on the moon started their migration in the last 100,000 years.

I have always been fascinated by this story: the rise and fall of entire species. Other humans perished: the Neanderthals, *Homo erectus* and *Homo floresiensis*. Anthropologists and geneticists have identified traces of these peoples' DNA alive in us still today. It is a lingering marker of a time when rival bands first looked upon each other, competed for food, fought and killed and in some cases mated.

This was when my people first came to this land. To think about that: to think that when people emerged from the cradle of our creation in Africa searching for new places to belong, we found ours here. When the first footprints of my ancestors touched the northern shoreline of this land, humanity itself had crossed a threshold.

A small band of people had chanced themselves on the open waters beyond the Indonesian archipelago. It stands as among the first great sea voyages, described by one anthropologist today as the equal of the Apollo mission to the moon.

Scientists fill in the timeline of human occupation; clues found in caves and rock shelters and embers of long-extinguished fires, in the fossilised remnants of tools carved out of stone, in the fragments of the bones of people who lived and died here. With each discovery a new page is written, dates revised, antiquity measured in millennia. Ten thousand, 30,000, 60,000 years: it tells us what we have already known – we have always been here.

* * *

Today I see the footprints of my people everywhere. When I stop looking straight ahead and cease thinking of tomorrow I can finally see my country. I can touch every horizon and know that I am home.

The sun shines brightest where it peeks through the clouds on a distant canola yellow hill. The rocks are strewn across open fields in odd formations. Some are nature's doing, the random placement as the earth has stirred. Others, though, have been carefully placed, marking the sites of ceremonies where boys were sung into men.

And now I sit here with my boy, by the water. The air is filled with birdsong. In the stillness we can hear the flapping wings of a duck as it skims the water's surface. In the distance there is the barking of a dog. I want to take it all in.

The roots of the trees around us are deeper – far deeper – than the footprints of the new people who claimed this land two centuries ago. Their branches bend to the banks of this waterhole. The trunks of other trees, now dead, lie submerged in the water. They are stark and lifeless. Their branches are stiff, white and bare, reaching like arms outstretched above the water's edge.

I tell my son that our people are buried here too. Their bones are lost somewhere in the creek bed. They died here too, like the trees. They perished here, deaths brutal and torturous.

I learned this story from my father and now I tell my boy. It is a story about how the ancient traditions and the deep connection to this land – all of it formed over thousands of generations – was smashed by the coming of people we called the Wandang, the ghosts. We are connected to this time and place and we are yet to emerge from its shadow.

In the 1830s the settlers and local Wiradjuri people – my father's people, the largest nation in the eastern seaboard – were locked in a cycle of violence. Frontier diaries and the writings of missionaries report sightings of bands of armed Wiradjuri warriors as they drove off or speared cattle and attacked homesteads. This pattern of guerrilla warfare had played out in other parts of Wiradjuri country. Here the response of the whites was the same: vigilante groups were formed to hunt us down.

At this waterhole my people took shelter and drank from the stream. They would return and leave as they had always done. But the waterhole was no longer theirs. British law had stripped them of their rights. To the settlers this land was empty and now it belonged to them. The local homestead owner wanted the blacks gone. He laced this waterhole with poison. Men, women and children died. Their bodies were left strewn along the banks rotting in the sun, a warning to others.

Their deaths linger here. I can feel it whenever I am home. It is not hard to picture them: bodies bent and twisted; mouths open; the air filled with the stench of vomit as they coughed up the poison. Flies hover over the decomposing flesh. Soon the birds will come to peck at the carcasses. There is no one to bury them. Here they will stay until they sink into the earth.

The killing didn't stop at this creek. Other Wiradjuri people fled to an island in the middle of the Murrumbidgee River. They huddled together and took shelter. The settlers and soldiers tracked them from the riverbank. When they came into view they aimed their guns and opened fire. All were killed, except for one boy. My father told me how this boy, with one eye blown out, floated downstream underwater, breathing through a hollow reed. Today this place too has a name: Murdering Island.

Poison Waterholes Creek, Murdering Island: to my people, these signs are literally tombstones. They mark the tragedy here. They remind us that this land was not settled peacefully. Whatever white Australians may have been told, these signs tell them too that we were here. We lived. We had families. This country was not empty.

This has become part of our dreaming. Once we would have told stories of creation, of the god Baiame who came down from the sky and made the rivers and mountains and forests. He made the first initiation site – the sacred Bora ground where boys became men. Now our stories are of people who came from another land and took what was ours.

I learned these stories at the feet of my parents. They told me other things: how they lived when they were young; what happened to their parents and their grandparents. I learned that we had survived; that we were still here. The spirits of our ancestors were still here.

This is what it means to be an indigenous person. It is what it means to be a Wiradjuri man. We have a place and a sense of place. It is what we ask each other when we meet another indigenous person. We don't ask who are you? We ask, where are you from? Where is your country?

This is why I have brought my son here to this waterhole. This is part of his country. These stories are his stories. I want him to be able to really see the rocks and the hills. I want him to feel the soil under his feet. I want him to open his ears to the sounds of his place. I want him to know the answer when one of his countrymen asks: where are you from?

I don't want him to be haunted with the images of death. I hope he can picture too, our people laughing by the creek. I hope he can see children like him ducking under the water. I hope – like me – he still hears the old sounds of singing and stamping feet. But we cannot ignore either, what happened here. The blood – our blood – that has stained the ground connects us to this darker time. It is a time that shadows black lives still.

I take his photo by the sign that reads: Poison Waterholes Creek. His eyes stare directly at the camera. He doesn't smile. He will again, as I smile, as do his grandparents. There is joy in being among each other. There is wonder in the world, and the world is his. But when he passes by this place he will know where he is from and he will know what happened here.

The next morning we leave early for the city. There is work and school and the rhythm of a life that sweeps us along. The sounds of the traffic will drown out the birds. We won't wonder at the strangeness of rocks or the markings on the trees. This has been my pattern: I come and I go, sometimes far away. But a sound and a smell can take me home and make me young again.

As we drive past the waterhole, over the bridge and that sign the sun is rising in the distance. The air outside is still and the last of the winter chill is hanging on the breeze. There is a long low mist shrouding the creek. It winds around the trees and trails off over the open paddock. The mist hovers less than two metres from the ground: about the height of a person.

* * *

My son is asleep now in the backseat and I am lost in my memories of the road. I love travelling: it is the movement more than the destination. I have always felt freedom here, with space around me, and distance in front of me.

This is the story of my life, a life spent looking out a window. As a boy I always felt reassured and comforted, especially at night in a car with the stars around me. I would prop myself up on my knees and stare out the back watching the white roadside posts pass by.

Inside it was warm, my brothers and sister were squeezed in tight, asleep. I could hear the murmur of my parents' conversation from the front seat. My father running a bottle top over the grooves of the steering wheel creating a rhythmic percussion that helped keep him awake.

Occasionally the darkness would be punctured by the red tinge of a cigarette as my mother lit up, inhaled and passed it over to my father. She has never been a smoker but she seemed to savour those moments; those little ceremonies; rituals of love and intimacy between two people, together facing up to the world.

I was always lost in thought. I thought about our family, how we moved from town to town with all that we owned inside our car. I eagerly awaited the next town: a new beginning. Maybe this would be it; maybe this would be the place we would finally stop.

We had all been born in different towns, my siblings and I. Each one: a dot on the map across western New South Wales. Every time would be the same pattern. Dad would get a job, we would find a house, Mum would go to the local charities – Smith Family, St Vincent de Paul – to get beds, blankets, clothes. I would start school with the same apprehension and trepidation, knowing no one, just a new boy walking into a playground where kids had already made their memories.

I remember my dad always saying the same thing, 'Home kids', as if this was our final stop. But just when I thought I might like it here we would move again. Dad would come home one afternoon Mum would load up the car. We'd take our clothes, nothing else. Everything would be left inside and we'd head out for the next town: the next beginning.

There are so few photos of me from school because I was never at any one place long enough to have them taken. I enrolled in more than a dozen schools before I was even in my teens; sometimes weeks, even months would go by when I barely saw a classroom. There was a time when I swapped my lessons for a fruit bucket and the back of a truck with my father and weeks travelling, selling door to door.

My love of books formed a buffer against my sporadic school years. I read whatever I could find. My mother always joked that I was 'old in the head'. I could read before I started school. I would grab what I could from libraries or old discarded books in second-hand stores.

I recall stories of myths: the names of Icarus, Achilles and Narcissus. I devoured great writers: Twain and Steinbeck and Hemingway, and from England, Dickens. Later still I discovered James Baldwin the black American writer – most important of all to me – who spoke to who I was: he helped bolster my identity and set my mind ablaze.

But my school report cards would never reflect this love of learning. I could never settle in long enough to find any consistency. On and on we moved, from one ramshackle house to another. The years passed sleeping in the backs of cars or crammed into an old plywood gypsy caravan.

My memory flashes through a slide show of snapshots that are my own personal calendar marking the years. I recall the sound of rats scurrying across a bare wood floor at night, a bucket catching the rain of a leaky roof, my brothers snuggled around me as we warmed ourselves in a shared bed against a bitter wind that crept through the gaps in the walls.

I can still hear the sound of my grandfather singing loudly and banging into the fence as he staggered home from a night on the drink, and my father lying in a bath, the water more like molasses darkened from blood and sap from his hours at work in a sawmill, his eyes closed and his body aching from the pain of survival.

Our family would expand and contract as we wove our journey: uncles, aunties, grandparents, cousins; we'd pick them up, they'd stay awhile and then peel off at the next town or the one after, in and out with the seasons. All of this to a soundtrack of old country music songs: songs of heartache and loss and yearning and being somewhere just below, always looking up at the lives we saw around us.

I would see Dad sitting for hours; his eyes closed and his head bent. He would be listening to Merle Haggard sing the story of my father's life; songs of hungry eyes and canvas-covered cabins, swinging doors, barstools, lonesome whistles and the day he started loving again. And my father would sing along.

Here was my education, more profound and indelible than anything taught in a classroom. These were lessons in what it takes to endure. I learned what it was to lead lives of dignity and meaning; how to wrest humour from despair. And how my family could laugh, and how I loved hearing them: those little moments the world could not touch.

I would watch my mother gently brush her hand on the back of my father's neck and see the hardness of his body soften, a yearning form in his eyes and a smile – faint and subdued – but tender. For those few seconds they'd allow the burden to ease just enough to give them the will to lift it again. I'm sure they weren't aware I even noticed, but I did; and I saw them say without need of words: this is it, this is what we have and no one is taking it.

Always I wondered about us, who we were and what put us here. I was aware always that we were marked by something more than poverty; that no amount of hard work, honesty or decency would untether us from our destiny. We lived in Australia and Australia was for other people.

If those people struggled too and if they suffered too then they did so knowing that this country was theirs. They could tear it down and build it back and force it to their will, they could go on strike or go to war; they could vote down governments; they could grasp the dream – the Australian dream – to raise themselves up and through it all they would be Australians. Even migrants came here as 'new Australians', tested and taunted yes, but in a generation: Australians. But not us; Australia we were told was settled and so was our fate.

So I worried about us and I feared for my family. I stayed close to my grandfather, hours sitting with him hearing him grind his teeth as he read old cowboy novels or listened to horse races on the radio, sharing the bitter dark chocolate he was fond of.

I helped my mother, trying always to be dependable, taking what money we had to fetch what she needed from the shop and counting the loose change. And I looked out for my father, a constant knot in my stomach, terrified of the danger of this world and how it could take him. He had felt the pain of being a black man in Australia. He knew it was a violent place. I knew that we could not survive without him.

I am formed more fully from these early years than all the decades that have followed. This is where I came into the world and it has never left me. The small boy I was is nestled deep in the man I have become. My own path – my people would call it my songline – has taken me far from the dark back roads of poverty and fear.

I remember them all: the people and places. There are faces and names that have mattered to me. Some are lost in time and I will never again see them. Others are dead. They have gone too soon: so young. For indigenous Australians this is the order of things.

I carry all of this and all of them in me. I will forever be a boy in a world suspended in time; a world back there. In those years our lives were an adventure. I would seek the little things that could lift my life from the poverty that surrounded me. I could suck the sweet nectar from flowers, taste the sweetness of honey from hives; swim in pools with the sun burning my back. We spoke loud and laughed hard. There was love and the feel of skin, mine on theirs and theirs on mine. In those moments I could hold my thoughts; I could push the questions of our lives aside. For that time – just that brief time – I was complete.

Life moved around me and through me. I could sit at a window on a sunny day and feel the warmth until my eyes gently closed. When I close them now I can imagine how it was. I see myself on a step outside a house in a small town. I don't have to be anywhere else. There's a gate and across the road a park. The street outside leads straight to town where there's a café and ice cream and a bakery and bread. I have a scooter, a good one with white pump-up tyres and it will take me there.

I hear the voices of those people now gone. I can hear my grandfather giving me a fright, grabbing me suddenly when I'm not expecting it. I hear my mother when she was young. I hear my father singing. I hear my brothers and my sister as we were then, before the world changed us.

I want to keep my eyes closed, clench them tighter. I want to stay there. I want to hold onto that minute in a restless life, and remember how it made me smile. I have never smiled so naturally again. I want to keep my eyes closed because I did not know then what I know now.

But I open my eyes and I am older than my grandfather was then. It isn't just the years that I measure. I have filled the years with distance. I have gone so far from that time and a window and the sun and those voices.

Now, I see that time differently; I see it how it really was. I remember being poor. I remember going to town and looking in those shops and wishing I could go in. I remember eyeing off a plastic football and wishing we could afford it and then going home and rolling some old socks into a ball with tape and using that instead. I remember that scooter as it was: older and more beaten. I remember that house: cold and rundown.

Closing my eyes and wishing memories away – imagining a different world – doesn't alter the past. Australia was hard on us. We came from a long line of people who had been battered. These people found themselves outside the grand sweep of this country's progress. We were black and Australia was white.

These are the thoughts that pass through my mind now as I drive with my son. I think of how I was at his age, and how different his life is. He is like his brothers and sister. They are strong and secure. They don't know the feeling of that knot-in-the-gut poverty. They don't know that life can be determined by prejudice. My son has known schools all over the world. He has sat in classrooms with friends from China and the Middle East. He dreams of going to America and becoming a basketball star, like his heroes Michael Jordan or LeBron James.

Between my son's life and mine is the Australian dream. This is the promise that with hard work, some talent and luck anything is possible. We are told this is the country of a fair go and mateship. It is a young country free of the troubles of old lands. For so many, this may be true. I recall hearing a woman interviewed who had studied the migrant experience. She found that within a generation difference becomes a virtue. We absorb cultures and customs. We change the food we eat, the music we listen to, the books we read. Our faces and names change. In this way we become Australians.

Outside my window, I am entranced by the way this land rises and falls. I see houses nestled in valleys. I see gates with names on them and winding dirt tracks. People work in the fields, their tractors throwing up dust, their skin burned brown like this land. I have met these people; many of them have a deep love of this country. They have begun to see it as we do. Wherever their ancestors may have begun their journeys it is here that these people have been formed.

This is where the Australian dream lives. It is in the roots of families who trace their heritage here back generations – sometimes to the First Fleet – and others who have just arrived to build a new life in a free, tolerant and rich land.

Black American writer Ta-Nehisi Coates has said of the American dream that it exists in ice-cream socials and Fourth of July cookouts. I see the Australian dream in shopping malls and coffee shops. It is in cinemas and playgrounds. The dream lives in the beach and the outback: it is a tourist brochure.

We advertise the dream on television. It is in the smile of a young blonde-haired girl driving a new car. The dream is a mother and father and a girl in pigtails carrying a doll, turning the key in the front door of their new home.

On weekends I get up close to the dream. It is on the sidelines at my sons' football games. Fathers, in loafers and boots and checked shirts and sweaters. It is in steak sandwiches and beers. It is in how comfortable they are with each other, regardless of where they hail from.

They welcome me. Yet in a deep, fundamental way they are strangers. As close as I get I still can't become one of them. I can count them as friends. I can smile, I can stop and chat but deep down I also know we are speaking a different language. The fault is as likely mine. There is a chasm here and I am not yet ready to cross. We occupy the same land, but we tell ourselves very different stories.

They tell themselves this is a great country of good people.

Here is how we – indigenous people – see the Australian dream: here's the worst of it. Aborigines rounded up and shot, babies buried into the sand and decapitated, women raped, men killed as they hid in the forks of trees, waterholes poisoned, flour laced with arsenic. The Australian dream abandoned us to rot on government missions, tore apart families, condemned us to poverty. There was no place for us in this modern country and everything we have won has come from dissent, it has been torn from the reluctant grasp of a nation that for much of its history hoped that we would disappear.

We know this history, my people. This is a living thing. We touch it and we wear it. It is written in the scars on the bodies of men like my father. It is carried deep within us, mental wounds that cannot heal. It is so close we can touch it.

When I was a baby my grandfather held me in his arms; he was the son of a man born onto the frontier before the collection of colonies even became Australia. A frontier marked with violence, disease and death. From me to my grandfather to his father: that's how close it is.

Being good and great does not absolve you from a terrible sin and a pain inflicted on a people who did nothing to deserve it. Remember that: the first people of this land who have suffered for your greatness did nothing to deserve it. A truly great country – if we truly believe that – should be held to great account.

Watching my son sleep, hearing his steady breathing as we move through our land calms me. I could be alone forever in these moments, surrounded by my country and with the boy whose bloodline through me stretches back an eternity. We are together in our place and I am aware that it may seem as if I have defied history. But we never do: do we?

PART TWO

I was born into what anthropologist W.E.H. Stanner called the 'great Australian silence'. It was the period of forgetting. The myths we created fed Australia's lie: that no blood had stained the wattle. We were told a story of peace and bravery and the conquest of a continent. This was the inevitable push into the interior, a land opening up before the explorers. It was empty; tamed and claimed.

These were the myths of my childhood, the myths of my education. In this telling, Australia was discovered by Captain James Cook. The *Endeavour* was a ship of destiny that led to the First Fleet. On 13 May 1787 eleven ships set sail with a cargo of prisoners to found a penal colony in New South Wales – but the true first fleet landed here 60,000 years earlier. I was told Lawson, Blaxland and Wentworth were the first people to cross the Blue Mountains.

There were people standing on the shore as Cook weighed anchor. Smoke from campfires trailed the white men who trekked over the great mountains west of Sydney;

black people watched these people who appeared like ghosts. But that story wasn't told in my classroom. The lesson I learned was that we didn't matter. In fact we didn't even exist.

I was young when I began to question all of this. Even through the eyes of a boy the glory of Australia did not match with the reality of our lives. Something was rotten here. Each morning at school I would stand in line to recite the pledge: I honour my God, I serve my Queen, I salute the flag. And then, in the evening I would return home to where this flag had deposited us. Home was wherever we could find it. It was a home on the margins, outside of town, outside looking in.

Here, was my place, among the detritus of the frontier: the huddled remnants of the hundreds of nations who formed here as the continent formed around them. Two thousand generations of civilisation and culture, all of it now smashed against the reality of white settlement, a people whose land was taken because the people themselves were not legally here.

School told me we faded from the frontier. The dying pillow was smoothed to soften our inevitable extinction.

It need not have been this way. The birth of Australia was meant to be so different. For a brief moment there was hope. Captain Arthur Phillip founded a penal colony with instructions from the crown to protect the lives and livelihoods of Aboriginal people and forge friendly relations with the natives. There were reports of blacks and whites dancing together with joy in the early days of the settlement. The local people began teaching their language to the newcomers. Here's what we could have been. In this moment there was a glimpse of a better Australia, and we failed.

Within a matter of years violence had broken out on both sides and Phillip would now instruct raiding parties to bring back the severed heads of the local warriors. Within a generation the heads of Aborigines were shipped back to Britain in glass cases, to be studied as relics of a doomed race.

Enlightened people throughout the world were wrestling with ideas of humanity and civilisation. The notion that all men are created equal was alive in the world. The 'immortal declaration' – as it was known – had been penned by Thomas Jefferson at the birth of America's independence a decade before the First Fleet arrived on these shores.

Yet, such lofty ideals had no place here. Not for us. We were dismissed as brutes. We were deemed to be the living example of what seventeenth century philosopher Thomas Hobbes meant when he spoke of the natural state as being 'solitary, poor, nasty, brutish and short'.

At best to some we were the 'noble savage'. We belonged to those so-called primitive people uncorrupted by civilisation. Yet such relics were seen to have no place in a modern world. The great writer of his age Charles Dickens spoke for many when he described such peoples as cruel, bloodthirsty and murderous. In Dickens' words we were whistling, clucking, tearing savages that he wished civilised off the face of the earth.

Charles Darwin – the father of the theory of evolution – visited Australia and despaired at the impact of colonisation. There was some 'mysterious agency', he said, that meant that 'wherever the European has trod, death seems to pursue the aboriginal [sic]'. There was of course nothing mysterious at all in the theft of land and the disease and violence that followed. Yet to Darwin – as sad as our passing may be – this was unavoidable, inevitable. His theories were born out of a belief in our common humanity but his name was linked to a popular acceptance of a hierarchy of races where the stronger trumps the weaker: 'Social Darwinism'.

How easy it can be in the sweep of history to stop seeing the individual lives. These were my ancestors they were speaking of, my great-great-grandparents. Such views formed a powerful logic that was unshakeable. It provided the moral blindfold through which people could no longer even see the atrocities perpetrated on my people. Even those people, whose eyes were opened to this suffering, accepted that our fate was doomed.

My ancestors were driven to the brink of extinction. We survived – the half-white remnants of the first nations herded onto Christian missions. We were told this would save us from the brutality of the frontier. But we often lived like inmates, roped and tied if we dared escape.

Now, I was a confused young boy at school, ashamed of what I was. I would cringe against the black and white ethnographic films: the snot-smeared faces of the little 'piccaninnies', the flyblown women grinding seed into flour, the bedraggled, bearded men gripping a spear, one leg resting against a knee. I remember there was always a narrator with perfectly rounded vowels telling of the 'once proud tribes of Aborigines'. Each head turned to look at me, and I felt anything but pride.

I saw my reflection in Australia and felt diminished. Everything told me I wasn't equal. The whites told the story of this land now; there was no glory in us. There was nothing that redeemed my ancestors. In books proudly titled *The Making of Australia* – a key school text of the 1960s – we were dismissed as the 'dark-skinned wandering tribes who hurled boomerangs and ate snakes' not fit to be counted in the glorious tale of white men and women who found the land, explored it, and made it a nation.

Back then no one wrote of our great deeds. If we existed at all, we were a footnote, a prehistoric relic. I was told the tragic story of the original Tasmanians and how they supposedly vanished from the earth.

My school history books carried photos of Truganini. At first she was young, proud and defiant and then older, grey, in a white woman's clothes. It was this later image that illustrated the fate of her people; how in one lifetime – I was taught – they had faded from the landscape. Of course that too was a lie, a tragic convenient version of history where guilt could be buried with the 'last Tasmanian'.

The Tasmanian blacks, just like us were clinging onto life, regrouping and replenishing on sparsely inhabited islands, the mixed offspring of whalers and Aboriginal women, with facial features that merged both and lighter skin, but outcast all the same and now told they were extinct.

* * *

Exclusion and difference: these were the abiding lessons of my early school years. They could be days marked with ritual humiliation. I can still hear the roll call of our names. One by one the black kids were pulled out of class. We'd be searched for head lice, our teeth examined. Our fingernails examined for signs of dirt. We were questioned about what we'd had for dinner the previous night. We would have to open our bags to show what we had for lunch.

I remember my teacher looking on and smiling as the government officers continued their interrogation. I recall grasping for answers. I did not know if I could satisfy them. These people likely thought themselves well meaning. But they scared me. My family – like any Aboriginal family – had seen children taken. It could just as easily be me. I remember after school, peering around my street corner looking for the tell-tale white cars of the welfare men, as we called them. Any sign of them and I'd hide out for hours. I would wait until dark then creep back home.

This is where I met white people. I met them in their imaginations. I was introduced in the snickering glances of my classmates, in the interrogation and implicit threat of the deceptively kind welfare officers and the complicit smiles of a kindergarten teacher who asked me to sing Cat Stevens songs for my class but was herself trapped in the prism of racism in 1960s Australia and could not see that morning had not broken for us.

I had no illusions of equality. We were another class of people. Our poverty branded on us as clearly as our colour. I wore the hand-me-down clothes of other people, pulled from cardboard boxes in second-hand bins. There were frayed, ill-fitting shirts, and jumpers stinking of mothballs with the names of other boys stencilled in the collars.

Like any childhood memories mine are sketchy. There are flashes of faces, perhaps a smell or a sound. Petula

Clark's 'Downtown' is a blast of musical liberation stuck on permanent rotation in my mind with its promise of forgetting our troubles and cares. I saw the movie *Born Free*, entering the cinema and being transported to Africa, a lion and freedom.

And I remember pineapple juice from a Golden Circle can. I can picture the two triangles punched in the lid to release the taste of a world of possibilities. I was probably five years old, and in one sip all of my senses were jolted to life. My small hands folded around the can. I can still smell that tangy, sticky, sweetness. Then there was the taste: an explosion on my tongue like a bee sting.

I only took one sip. It was my father's juice, his one indulgence. It was the small piece of the world he'd hold for himself, a reward for bending his back to put food on our table. My mother warned us not to touch it. But like any child that only made it more tempting. In one forbidden sip I tasted the promise of a world outside my own; a world of music and movies that shone so brightly but were ultimately counterpoints to a more grim reality. The abiding memories of my childhood remain the things that separated us.

On my seventh birthday my mother threw me a party. It was the only birthday party I ever had as a child. Where she got the idea or imagined we could afford it I don't know. Many meals in our house were rounded out with food begged off charity agencies. My mother and grandmother would make the rounds of the Smith Family or Salvation Army. Along with a 'God is love' sticker would come a food voucher to cover the bare essentials.

But I was a good boy, my mother's helper. She could trust me. I'd help her clean. I would run to the shop, chop wood or help with my younger siblings. I guess she just thought I deserved a little party. She poured some cordial into paper cups and sprinkled some hundreds and thousands onto white bread and made some chocolate crackles. She set it all on a park bench and asked me to invite some kids from school.

I can recall so clearly, how I felt. It is a feeling that has never left me. No amount of education, travel and prosperity can ever erase it. I was sick with fear. I had a headache – as a child I was plagued with sickening headaches – and a pain in my gut. I thought these kids would laugh at me. Worse than that I was afraid that they would laugh at my beautiful, kind, loving mother.

These fears, the fear of being laughed at, the fear of being caught out wearing another boy's cast-off clothes, the fear of the welfare men, all of this marked the territory between the world of Australia and me. This was the space that history had made and the place it had reserved for people like us.

* * *

I was fourteen when I confronted the world that awaited me. I stood sickened and transfixed, repulsed yet unable or unwilling to look away. Others were ready – eager even – to embrace this world. Violence was where we proved ourselves. There was status and glory here. My friends and I measured ourselves on our ability to fight. But on this day I was shocked and stunned and I have carried that memory with me forever.

I recall this scene with a soundtrack of hissing and spitting and heaving and the crack of bone and the heavy dull thud of a fist sinking into that soft skin below the ribcage. There were other people yelling and cheering and others still entangled in their own swinging fists and pulling of hair. The fight had broken out among rival Aboriginal families after a day of drinking at the local showground. But I watched only two men, both black, one of them my older cousin.

Maybe it was because this was my blood, my kin, that it was so much more horrifying and maybe I saw something that was in me too. My cousin had the other man, a much bigger, heavier set man, against a wall; the only thing that kept the other man upright was the rapid-fire piston-like punches of my cousin. His hands had the power of set cement. In my mind it lasts an eternity but perhaps it was over in minutes. In the end the bigger man was coughing blood from his mouth.

What I saw went beyond violence; it was a rage born of history. The whites had thrown us together, potently mixing family, clan and law and we had turned in on each other. We unleashed a fury on ourselves that came from powerlessness. We often hear the term 'black on black crime': but it is just crime. Our victims are our neighbours and they are black.

I had my own taste of violence around this same time. My local high school was divided into black, white and Italian. It was a self-imposed segregation that defined where we sat, who we ate with and which football team we played for. I would break solidarity and walk home with an Italian boy whose family ran the local pizza shop. Occasionally he would sneak me one.

Some white kids liked to sit with us and befriended us, copying the way we spoke and laughed. We tolerated it, to a point. But when fights broke out we knew which side we were really on. One day it came to me to show my allegiance and I was goaded into brawling with one of the white boys who hung with us. Violence doesn't come naturally to me. Some people are born to it. I have seen that. But as much as it scared me, I realised that day that the rage in my cousin, that I had seen in others in my family, was in me too.

This was a time of coming of age in 1970s Australia. The country town I then lived in was like all the others I'd moved between. Young men with their first cars drove up and down the main street; endless looping laps hour after hour. We would meet at the swimming pool, diving and dunking each other. If we had gathered enough discarded bottles we could cash them in for spare change, enough to buy a bag of lollies at two for a cent. Then we'd sun ourselves on our stomachs on the baked hot cement around the pool.

If we couldn't afford the price of admission to the pool we would make do with cooling off in the many irrigation channels that ran through my town. One of them passed through the Aboriginal mission where my relatives lived. The bridge that crossed it split in three directions and the mission became known as 'the Three Ways'.

Home for me was a government housing commission development just up from the mission, in what had previously been another 'blacks camp' known as Frogs Hollow. We were at the very edge of town; we knew where the town ended because that's where the tar road finished. From the last of our houses a corrugated dirt track ran down to the mission and in all my childhood it was never sealed.

My house was next to my uncle's and our cousin's house was next to his. We were tossed together in a social experiment of blacks and whites bound by being poor. But we filled our time with football games and bike riding and playing marbles and stealing watermelons from the local farmers and floating them down the channels to where we'd boarded up makeshift dams. When everyone is poor you don't know you're poor. My father worked so some of the boys thought I was actually rich.

My father's grandmother – my great-grandmother – lived down at the mission. She was always an old lady to me. Her teeth were gone but she loved to suck the caramel out of the chocolates we would always bring with each visit. She loved to collect the pull tops from soft drink cans and wear them as rings. Nanny Cot, we called her; always surrounded by her grandchildren and now her great-grandchildren like me. Some she had raised herself after their parents had died. Nanny Cot outlived many of her kids.

My great-uncle lived behind her house in a caravan. He was my grandmother's brother and would spend a couple of nights a week with her in her house uptown. My grandfather had some land and he built a tin and fibro house before he died. When life on the mission would get too much my great-uncle could escape to be with his sister.

He would walk the couple of miles past the main irrigation channel to her home. One week he failed to turn up. A few days passed before his body was pulled from the water. Death could touch us at any time; it was random but never unexpected. We lost many people to the channels; slipping and falling in – some with too much to drink – unable to get out.

Nanny Cot was a living link to Australia's frontier history. She'd been born onto the Warangesda Mission on the banks of the Murrumbidgee River; founded by a crazed Rasputin-like preacher, John Brown Gribble, who had been rescued by Aborigines when he wandered off as a child on the Victorian goldfields. In his mind he would repay the debt by saving us from what he saw as the ravages of the colonial whites. Gribble described the blacks of the Murrumbidgee as 'a wretched focus of iniquity'.

But if Warangesda – meaning home of mercy – was meant to be our salvation it failed. It collapsed into a living hell and when the blacks would try to flee, the pastor would round them up on horseback and tie them together with rope and drag them back again. Gribble himself went slowly insane before the church shipped him to England, broken and tormented. He penned a book aptly titled *Dark Deeds in a Sunny Land*.

My great-grandmother now lived out her days on the Three Ways. We would visit each weekend and my grandmother from uptown would attend the mission church. This was a hard place. Barely half a kilometre separated me and where I lived and these houses – but it represented another world, a relic of the frontier. We were the lowest step on the awkward, tentative ladder of assimilation – we were the future; the mission, the past.

We were all blood relatives, but the boys on the mission seemed edgier and darker. The girls had a snarl and an attitude in their walk. Some of them had scratched rough, blue ink tattoos onto their arms: boys' names usually. The dogs looked a bit leaner and meaner, and we kicked the football on a dusty dry oval full of spiky burrs. The tough boys I played footy with eventually torched the church to the ground.

We would all catch the bus to the local high school. The blacks' bus, we called it. It was a time when the government was trying to encourage Aboriginal kids to stay in school. Each term my parents would get a cheque for books and uniforms. Each fortnight we kids would get a cheque of our own for three dollars. We'd know when it was our payday; all the kids on the blacks' bus would charge out near the school and make a beeline for the local shop to cash in.

Those years from thirteen to fifteen seem now like some sort of reprieve. Just for that time we were boys and girls. The pool was the pool and football was football. Yes, we were blacks and whites and we revelled in our segregation. But in a small town, we all knew each other and we all did the same things. The shade of the prison house had not yet fallen on our lives, but it was looming. Just then though, for that moment, potential and ambition did not seem so fanciful.

For those years from thirteen to fifteen we were invincible. Never again would we as black people be better than everyone else, be tougher than everyone else. There was status and pride in being Aborigines – Kooris – we could strut and laugh loudly.

White kids wanted to be us – not just with us – they wanted to talk like us and act like us. For that brief time we made the rules, we'd scoff how they thought they were blackfellas but they weren't. We didn't doubt who we were, we didn't have to justify it, we didn't even have to think about it. We were on land that was ours; we were blood our families weaved in and out of each other in intricate kinship. I have never known that certainty since.

These were untapped lives, kids full of cheek and wit. I didn't stand out at all as someone especially capable let alone remarkable. I was happy to go along, playing football, messing up in class, going to the pool. But I always watched and thought and wondered why our lives were so different from the whites' lives.

I would sit in the tree behind my grandmother's house just thinking of what else might be out there. Other boys were more handsome, better footballers, brighter students. Many of the girls were absolutely fearless and they gave off sparks of energy. These kids could have powered their communities. But the tyranny of low expectations smothered them.

When I was fifteen, the principal of our high school called some of us Aboriginal kids to his office. He wanted us gone. By law we were no longer required to attend school. He suggested it might be time we looked at other options. We could pick fruit or work on the local council. Some of us might get an apprenticeship, he said, but higher education was clearly not an option.

The government was paying us to try to keep us in school, but the headmaster was doing what missionaries, welfare officers and the police had been doing for two hundred years: he was handcuffing us to our history, reminding us that if we did have a place in Australia it would be on the margins. Here was my early taste of how official policy – well intended – could shatter against a wall of entrenched racism.

It is these moments – minutes in our lives but repeated over and over – which poison our souls and kill us as sure as the waterholes poisoned on the frontier killed our ancestors. It hasn't changed; laws can outlaw discrimination but they can also harden the bigotry in the minds of some people.

The light went out of the eyes of my cousins and schoolmates as they later limped from the classroom. Their bravado wouldn't allow them to show vulnerability. They flaunted their imagined freedom, adding another layer of defiance to their already hardened exterior. But quietly and inevitably whatever fire and spark had existed, now extinguished.

Their lives became like stagnant pools of water. With nowhere to run they were slowly polluted. It isn't that there is no joy. But it gets harder to find, until drink and drugs and violence fill those empty spaces. Not everyone suffers in this way; some find a rhythm of work and family and enough love to push out the confines of their lives. But those who don't make it die.

Funerals call me home far too often. My mother and father seem always to be telling me of another person who has passed away. For indigenous people, life can be a nearly constant state of mourning. If I walk through the graveyard of my hometown I see so many lives cut short. Kids I grew up with, cousins and uncles and aunts whose smiles are still fresh in my mind now lie beneath crosses marking their birth dates, people who would be only in their forties or fifties.

My cousin Lex lies here. As a boy I looked up to him. He had lost his parents – my grandmother's brother and his wife – when he was only young. My uncle and aunt took him in and raised him as theirs. I can remember sitting on his bed as he showed me his school Army Cadets uniform and his rifle. Big Lex, we called him. He always seemed stronger, more grown up even though he was no more than five years older than me. I was living in Beijing when my mother called to tell me he had died.

There is one funeral that has stayed in my mind. It was for another cousin, another man dead at just fifty years old. We sang 'The Old Rugged Cross' that day as we always do:

'On a hill far away stood an old rugged cross, the emblem of suffering and shame.' Our church was always big on sin and redemption: a church of the fallen. They were all there, my old friends and family. I looked at one man, studying his face. He was so familiar but changed. He was hard and lean; there were scars around his eyes. He was hollowed out and looked ten years older than me.

I had seen this man as a boy, curled up on his bed reading comic books. We had played football together, pairing up to gang tackle our opponents so hard they would break. There was one game where we took aim at a big boy on the other side. We smacked our hands together and looked at each other and zeroed in, one high one low. As the ball reached his hands we struck a perfect collision of bone on bone and we felt the air leave his body as he folded into the ground.

This boy I played football with and laughed with; this boy who was tricky and fast and smart; this boy made one false move. He listened when the principal told us to leave school. That man, thin and mean, who loved caning us especially in winter when it stung or bled. He didn't see our potential; he saw our colour. He set my friend on a path of mistakes that led to drugs and jail. Now he sat there barely recognisable to me. This is what Australia can do to black lives.

For that instant, maybe I was unrecognisable to him too. What plans we had made had never been expected to lead us to here. The boys that met as friends were strangers now. We were each left to our own mistakes. It is the conceit of success that the world of our childhood will remain suspended, just waiting for us to reconnect. We can return, laugh and remember and then move on, away from the world that made us to the new one we'd created.

Those who stay behind we expect to remain as we knew them, locked in a photo frame, a reflection of our simpler selves. But their lives turned too and for my friend it had turned hard. We did recognise each other after a minute, we hugged as boyhood friends do but we would never be those boys again.

A different fate beckoned me too. Somewhere in a parallel universe, maybe there were drugs and crime and jail. A sliding door into another life, a life measured in the grim statistics that can define my people: disease, unemployment, death. This life would never have taken me far from the limits of my hometown.

There are those who stayed and still lived quiet lives of dignity; perhaps that would have been me. But I will never know. Part of me is always there, but a greater part of me left. I cheated the odds and it all turned on luck and timing.

My father's restlessness took us away again. We left town, left my friends and family and moved to Canberra. My father had a job on a sawmill that paid a little more money. This was our way: we moved, we stopped then we moved again.

I don't know what drove Dad but I suspect it was the gambler in him. He would place his bet then double it again, hoping to cash in at the next town. He was a saw miller, a tree feller, a fruit picker; he laid concrete, detonated explosives and built dams. He was sinew and muscle, and that bought us shelter and food.

He was hard on me, or so I thought. He wouldn't spare the belt. These were lessons taught by his father and passed to me. Black men who knew the price black men could pay in this country. It felt like I was always in the corner of his eye and I wondered if I was also in his heart. If I strayed too far from view or looked to be nearing the dangerous edges of our world he would corral me and keep me in line; give me a taste of the consequences that might be waiting for me.

He knew the world better than me and he was preparing me for that world. It was a world where men settled arguments with their fists. He taught me how to fight too, moves and combinations he'd perfected in the travelling boxing tents.

We'd put on the gloves, he would put his hands up in front of me and show me how to throw a jab and snap it back straight to guard my face, how to crouch and dig my elbows into my midriff. He'd watch my feet and teach me to keep them just the right distance apart; too wide, he said, and I'd lose power and balance. He'd warn me to keep my eyes trained on my opponent. He showed me how to roll my shoulders to take the sting out of blows. But above all, he said, relax and breathe; a tense fighter is a fighter who has lost.

This was Marquess of Queensberry rules. The real battles when they came would be in the street, and he taught me those lessons too: how never to grab another man's shirt and lose the advantage of two hands. He told me if I was ever outnumbered to get in front of a wall so I could not be surrounded, and never, he said, allow myself to go to the ground or I would get a kicking.

My father couldn't refine my golf swing or show me how to set a sail or strengthen my backhand; he had no need of these things. Those lessons would count for nothing in the world he laid out for me.

I looked on my father's world with a mix of fear and love. I loved the tangy smell of him when he'd come home from the mill, how the sawdust would tickle my nose. I would go to the mill and see big men with muscles carved from hard work and heaving logs twice their size.

They'd break for smoko and twist the lids off flasks of sweet tea; heads bowed and shoulders slumped, beads of sweat tracing unshaven skins. They wouldn't speak much, maybe offer a cigarette and swish the last sip of tea around the bottom of their mugs before emptying it into the dirt and going back to work.

They were usually white, these hard men, but my father found a place there. He found brotherhood in poverty, in shared struggle, black and white. But for white people, being poor didn't define them in the way our blackness defined us. Poverty itself could be temporary and if by chance or effort they broke its chains, there'd be a white world waiting. But we would be black and that would always pose uncomfortable questions for Australia.

My father had pushed against the boundaries of blackness and knew it was safer living in the cracks. This is where we took refuge and he marked out territory with his body. I was wrong to wonder about my place in this man's heart. There wasn't a lot of room for sentiment but he squared up to the world and he took its hardest blows for us and he saved me from that fear that I felt every time I watched him at the mill, the fear that the world he lived in would crush me.

By the 1970s self-determination became the buzzword for Federal Government policy for Aborigines. Gough Whitlam had established the Department of Aboriginal Affairs. There were programs to try to keep kids in school, create employment and promote home ownership. This was an attempt to level the playing field, create pathways for Aboriginal families to merge more successfully with what we were told was 'mainstream Australia'. In Canberra my parents applied for an Aboriginal housing loan. Dad stashed away a small deposit, working overtime shifts at the mill; Mum earned extra cash cleaning cars in Canberra's frosty winter's mornings. It was work that would leave her red raw, cracked and bleeding. No more though, would we be rootless – no more rundown mill shacks or tiny caravans. My father could now settle on land and call it a home.

Now he had a place: his place. It meant change and it wasn't easy. I went from a school segregated by colour to a school where my sister and I were the only Aboriginal children. There was racism and hurtful taunts but I could reinvent myself and I made friends.

It sounds simple. Some would say this is the answer for us all. Leave, find a new life, work; avoid the clutches of poverty and despair. Former Prime Minister Tony Abbott described this as a lifestyle choice. If only that were all there was to it. When we move we don't just leave family, we leave country. If constantly moving made my family a smaller target, forever dodging racism and the heavy hand of the welfare men, then it also came at a cost. I always felt displaced and it could be lonely. I can't deny that the lure of a new town, a bigger city, gave us new hope but it didn't mean white Australia was not uncomfortable or unwelcoming. I learned that the price of acceptance was to smooth out my differences until I was almost in denial about being Aboriginal.

It is hardly surprising that some of our people prefer to stay where they are. Here is another uncomfortable, confronting question: who says we have to aspire to white Australia's idea of a good life? Sometimes defiance is all we have. We know the cost and have paid it and continue to pay it. While ever our communities are not empowered, without an economic base, the opportunity to build wealth, to strengthen ourselves on our own terms, then we face the daunting, sometimes insurmountable challenge of finding our place in a white world that we know can so easily and brutally reject us.

Alone in Canberra, away from the black cousins and friends who nourished my identity, I needed something to cling to. At school I could be the brown boy who played sport and liked music and never spoke much about being Aboriginal. The other kids knew what I was but no one really wanted to talk about it. But at home I found strength and a sense of moral outrage in the words of James Baldwin. I read *Go Tell It on the Mountain*, Baldwin's first novel. Here were people I knew, a struggle across the generations; religion and race.

Black America fascinated me. I looked to the Civil Rights movement, the oratory of Martin Luther King, the 'by any means necessary' fire of Malcolm X, the Nation of Islam or 'black Muslims' and the Black Panther Party. I had a poster of Tommie Smith and John Carlos, their gloved hands raised in a black power salute of defiance on the victory podium at the Mexico Olympics in 1968. These were people who stood up, and James Baldwin was their poet laureate.

I think I first borrowed it from the library, this book that would change my life. The name attracted me; I had always loved the song and its plea to 'let my people go'. Here was the story of a family and two brothers: Roy and John. Between them was a history of slavery and brutality. John's birthday triggered a rupture that laid bare the secrets, torment and pain all in the shadow of the cross. The book turned on the Oedipal drama of John's life. He looked for the love of his distant preacher father. Reconciling his own sin he embraced God.

But this was a family of secrets. John's father was not his father. He was the man who married John's mother and never let her forget it. In a final act of devotion John prostrated himself at the feet of the lord. It was an act of desperation and it mocked his father's hypocrisy.

How I loved the drama of these stories: the sweep of family and history. Baldwin's God was the God of redemption and punishment. The people of this book, trapped between sin and salvation, shaking with the force of temptation, inviting the fires of hell. These were the lives I saw around me too. My people had been 'saved' on the missions, delivered from sin and their own blackness.

Like Baldwin's characters we fell and were reborn. We were like John's father, the preacher Gabriel, straightened on the path of righteousness only to become punishingly sanctimonious. *Go Tell It on the Mountain* spoke to me with its story of children born in secret, of a woman banished to die young in shame, and a preacher commanding authority from the pulpit he could never replicate at home.

Go Tell It on the Mountain led to Baldwin's other books. In his essays 'Notes of a Native Son' and 'The Fire Next Time', Baldwin charted a course through the pain and humiliation of racism. He was blunt – brutally at times – and he told me: 'For the State, a Nigger is a Nigger is a Nigger, sometimes Mr. or Mrs. or Dr. Nigger.'

In a letter to his nephew James he warned: 'You can only be destroyed by believing that you really are what the white world calls a *nigger*.' I knew this. I had seen this. Being black – being Aboriginal – was intensely political. Our identities were a political statement; even denial of our identities was political.

Baldwin wrote with fluency and confidence. He did not compromise. There was no doubt. He accused America of the crime of destroying hundreds of thousands of black lives and not knowing it and not wanting to know it.

Later I would gain a deeper understanding of his work. I would learn of his struggle to express himself as a black man, as a gay man in America. I would learn of how he sought exile in Paris and saw his country even more deeply; more clearly, from afar. I had no inkling then that one day I would do the same.

* * *

Career, dreams, ambitions: these were foreign concepts to me. I had stumbled through school more focused on fitting in – playing football, learning guitar, going to rock gigs – than excelling. The years since I had left Griffith had passed by in a soporific haze; just one dreary season after another in suburban Canberra. We lived in what to others would have seemed just another dull grey brick veneer house in a nondescript street in a rather barren northern outpost of the city. The government had built thousands of these dwellings in the 1960s and 70s as part of a public housing boom. They were since sold off cheap and commonly referred to as 'ex-govies'. To me though, it was a palace. I even had my own room! Remember I had spent a lifetime squeezed into the same bed as my brothers and stepping over my grandfather to get outside.

I am tempted to call this part of Canberra colourless, but it wasn't: it was white. I was surrounded by the children of white middle-ranking public servants. We were as exotic as it got, save for a Middle Eastern Kurdish family who inexplicably turned up at my school only to find themselves ostracised and the butt of playground racist taunts. In my years there I recall rarely if ever inviting anyone over to my house. I preferred them at arm's length, this was a hangover from early childhood – jeers and stares – I didn't want to invite any more white judgment. One loud-mouthed boy once proclaimed how he'd seen my father on a bus and how black he was! As had become my custom I just shrank a little and hoped the mocking laughter would pass quickly.

It wasn't horrible – just a grinding monotony. I was simply another unremarkable youth in uninspiring 1970s Australia – just with a darker face than most were used to. I had some mates and filled in my time with a cricket ball, a football, hot days swimming in the tangled reeds of the lake, or wandering the floors of the new shopping mall. This was our haunt on Friday nights – up and down, in and out of shops in which I had no money to spend. I would save what I had for deformed donuts – the misshapen rejects that would be sold for fifty cents a bag. I would eat them as I listened to music through headphones in the record store. If I managed to earn some money mowing lawns, clearing rubbish or delivering papers I would usually spend it on music. I was caught up in the wake of the punk explosion in England; I loved the Sex Pistols, The Clash and especially The Jam. For a time I wore a parka like an English mod with a Union Jack pencilled onto it. One day a black man pulled me aside and asked with a sneer why I was wearing something like that. 'You aren't from there,' he said.

He was right. I had never truly felt a sense of belonging except back on the road in any of the small towns that had littered my childhood. I was without my grandfather for one thing. He had moved around with us but he didn't make it to Canberra. My parents came home one day and I watched them sit in the car before coming in, with my mother in tears and my dad telling us Pa had died. He wasn't even sixty years old. I ran out of the house and just kept running, refusing to accept this news. Travelling to his funeral I kept thinking how he would be there waiting for us alive and well. He still comes to me in my dreams sometimes.

Nothing was expected of me and I expected nothing of myself. After school I drifted into one job or another. I considered working in a shoe shop then ended up as a trainee at the Canberra Tourist Bureau, learning how to book and issue bus and train tickets and advise visitors on the highlights of our nation's capital: the War Memorial, Parliament House, the lake. After that they were on their own. I was totally uninspired and useless. I lasted there a few months but at least it gave me money to spend on more records. Before long I landed another job delivering internal mail at the Australian Institute of Aboriginal Studies (now the Australian Institute of Aboriginal and Torres Strait

Islander Studies – back then we were all just Aborigines).
Wasn't I going places!

This was a fateful move, one of many in my life. At the
Institute I reconnected with the kinship I had lost when we
moved to the city. There was a subterranean black community
lurking below this bland bush city. People had been lured here
to work in Aboriginal affairs, others to attend universities
whose affirmative action policies were opening doors for
black people. At the Institute my uncle – my father's cousin –
worked as a janitor. I would spend lunchtimes with him
laughing and eating just as I used to do with my grandfather.

I had drifted away from my few friends from school.
I had little truly in common with them anyway. They had
provided a few years of refuge and I am grateful, but there
was no lasting connection. Now my eyes were opened to
new possibilities. At the Institute there were people like
me – Aboriginal people – studying, writing and wrestling
with new ideas. These people worked as film and sound
archivists and anthropologists and historians. Black people
did this? I could barely believe it. The white people there too
were different, they were British and German and Dutch
and American; they weren't burdened with the history of
this country. They didn't want to hide the shame of our
past; they wanted to hold it up to the light.

James Baldwin said it best and it has remained with
me: 'History is a hymn to white people, and all us others

have been discovered'. Australian historians 'discovered' us in the 1970s. Over the next decade, they wrote books with titles like *Outcasts in White Australia*, *The Other Side of the Frontier*, *The Aboriginal Tasmanians*. New words filled my vocabulary: ethnocentrism, social Darwinism and genocide. I filled in the gaps in our history inspired by this darker tale of tragedy, of poisoned waterholes, arsenic-laced flour, decapitated bodies, babies buried alive, the black line in Tasmania, martial law in Bathurst, Truganini, Bennelong, smallpox, typhoid, leprosy, dysentery, scabies, the corrosive misery of sugar and grog, the rotting hell of missions, police bashings, swinging bodies in lonely cells, the whole godforsaken Aboriginal existence.

This was all part of Australia's emerging new sense of itself. This country had been grappling for decades with a shifting sense of our place in the world. Australian soldiers returned home from World War II to a country forever changed. Women had experienced work and their daughters would not so readily accept subservience. A new generation of migrants spilled out of the devastation of post-war Europe; Greeks and Italians made their way here, bringing new languages and food and customs. The nation that had gone to war in service to the Empire now turned from Britain to the new global superpower, the United States.

American soldiers had been based in Australia during the war and fought for the liberation of the Asia–Pacific region from the Japanese imperialists. They left behind their music and sprinkled old Aussie slang with new phrases. From now, Australia's destiny would be bound between Canberra and Washington. It was a union forged in blood and treasure in every conflict from Korea to Vietnam and Afghanistan and Iraq.

New languages, new faces, new names needed a new identity. Australians found a sense of themselves constructed from a narrative that wasn't necessarily wrapped in the Union Jack. I don't know when exactly, but it was around this time – the early 1970s – that my school dropped the morning pledge to serve the Queen, honour God and salute the flag. For me it meant not having to cross my fingers behind my back in silent childhood protest.

Decades of conservative rule ended with the election of the Whitlam government and its rapid program of social change. We were living in the 70s to a soundtrack of Skyhooks and Sherbet and *Countdown* on Sunday night television. This decade, we would be introduced to new phrases: multiculturalism and boat people and land rights.

Aborigines were swept along in this changing Australia. We came into clearer focus as the nation grappled with our place in this land. We were now counted in the census – no longer listed among the flora and fauna. There were more strident calls for equality and justice. A new generation of Aboriginal activists demanded compensation for what was now called the theft of our land and the massacre of our people. Where the previous generations of black leaders were drawn from the missions and churches, these new angry voices were fired by the black Civil Rights movement in America. They styled themselves in tribute to the Black Panthers and spouted the words of Malcolm X.

In 1972 these new black radicals pitched tents on the lawn of Parliament House. This was a protest aimed to shame. They wanted to throw into contrast the power on the hill and the suffering of fringe dwellers. In the words of Aboriginal journalist, John Newfong, the mission had come to town. This was my introduction to politics. My big cousin Bob McLeod, a ferocious, intensely charismatic man, pitched his tent too. He wrote songs and sang them beautifully. He pulled his long hair back with a red headband.

Later, he would hold up the Department of Aboriginal Affairs with a gun as the Queen was opening parliament. For now, I would peer at him from behind my bedroom door whenever he would visit. I was always a little awed and intimidated by this big presence with his strong voice and the way he would call my mother and father 'sister' and 'brother'. This was a new militant unity. It was an expression of black will that Australia had not seen since the days of resistance on the frontier.

All community is in some way imagined. We attach ourselves to our story, seeing our reflection in each other. French writer and philosopher Michel De Certeau speaks of history as the gesture of new beginnings. Reading his work took me backstage in the production of my own identity.

In this way I'm not so different from you. We look to popular culture to fortify our sense of who we are. Music, books, films lend poetry and lyricism and character to our lives. This is a bigger canvas to recreate ourselves, as we would have ourselves seen. On this stage we would liberate our stories from the leaden pages of academia and infuse them with heroics and courage and triumph.

In the 1970s Australians rediscovered a foundation myth. The story of Gallipoli was reimagined. No longer was it a defeat. It was now a transformative event that forged an identity that encompassed the best of what we believed about ourselves. In this new telling the Diggers landed on the Turkish beaches as soldiers of the British Empire but those who survived, left as Australians.

While trying to find a place in white suburban Canberra I also found a counter-narrative in a film of the 1970s, Fred Schepisi's *The Chant of Jimmie Blacksmith*. This was the story of an Aborigine who fought back. He tore off the white shirt of the missionaries and stained it red with the blood of settlers. Schepisi drew the story from a novel by Thomas Keneally, but this was thinly disguised history.

Jimmie Blacksmith was based on a very real black outlaw: Jimmy Governor. He was part white with a white wife but it won him no acceptance. Jimmy and Ethel were taunted for their interracial marriage and mixed-blood child.

The real Jimmy had found work on a farm near Dubbo in western New South Wales owned by the Mawbey family. The Governors were allowed to live on the property. But it was an uneasy coexistence. Ethel complained of abuse and there were disputes over food and rations. On a cold winter night on 20 July 1900, Jimmy took revenge. With his uncle Jacky Underwood, he bludgeoned to death five people – women and children – with tomahawks and nulla-nullas.

The farmhouse was a scene of strewn bodies. Floors and walls were splattered with blood. Jimmy and his uncle fled, killing others as they escaped and leaving bodies on the roadside. They embarked on a campaign of robbery and murder and sparked the biggest manhunt to that time in Australian history. It was a crime spree that collapsed the brutal settlement of Australia and the dispossession of the original people with the birth of a new nation on the cusp of federation.

Through Schepisi's lens Jimmie Blacksmith became a freedom fighter. A black man pushed to breaking point by a country that had stolen his people's land. It had tempted the white blood in him and then rejected him anyway. It was a beautifully imagined film. The serene landscape of rolling hills and open plains juxtaposed with the brutality of what had played out here: atrocities both black and white.

In Tom E. Lewis, an untrained actor, Schepisi found his vision of Jimmie. He had a wide grin, and friendly eager eyes that then transformed into rage and confusion. In the film's overtly political high point, Jimmie learns of Australians fighting in South Africa's Boer War and declares: 'That's what I've done, I've declared war. Declared war!' That last word 'war' echoing through the valley as symbolic white cockatoos scatter below.

Of course this powerful, violent and defiant film would resonate with a fifteen-year-old Aboriginal boy raised on a history of black submission and defeat. My brothers and I would repeat scenes from the movie, teasing my mother: 'Yes, boss. No, boss. Three bags full, boss. I'll be a good black fella for you, boss.'

This was not just a movie. I had a real connection with these events. Jimmy Governor was a Wiradjuri like me. The Governor family lived alongside my father's family at an Aboriginal mission.

* * *

Here I was now at the Institute library surrounded by books I never knew existed, so many books about my people. I read voraciously. In between my mail rounds or photocopying I would spend hours searching through the Institute's archives. Here were old colonial records, the diaries of missionaries and settlers and the notes of welfare agencies. My entire family's history was held in these files. I would enter a name and find the details of their birth, where they lived, what the mission managers said about them, where they worked, who they married, sometimes police records and how and when they died. There were old photographs – black and white images of ancestors I had been told about but had never seen. Once, I was taken into a cold storage area to see secret and sacred objects and was shown a shield and a boomerang that had been made by one of my father's great uncles. It was a magical place where I could touch my past.

I was in the library one day when one of the Aboriginal researchers approached me. Marcia Langton was one of the first black students at the Australian National University; she was studying anthropology and history. Marcia was always a fearsome sight. She had a reputation for being brutally direct and seemed intimidated by no one. She had been involved in the Aboriginal political movement and belonged to a new generation who would not allow white Australia to define them.

Marcia sat me down and in her own no-nonsense way asked what I thought I was doing with my life. She told me I had a greater future than spending my days behind a mail trolley. She asked what I wanted to be. I told her I would like to be a journalist and it is true that I had always been fascinated by news. I read the papers every day, front to back and watched the television bulletins, but I had no idea that it was something I could aspire to. Marcia encouraged me to consider university and within a couple of days was back with enrolment forms and helped me fill them out. I was accepted to the University of New South Wales and within a few months crossed a threshold that no one in my family had previously even imagined.

At university I found unity in my fellow black students on campus. In 1981 there would barely have been a dozen of us. We shared our family's histories. We swapped genealogies, finding connections in our family trees. I talked politics with closest mates – Don Jenner, a law student who I came to love as a brother and Warren Mundine, now senior indigenous adviser to the Prime Minister. Back then we were impatient and angry young men. We marched in demonstrations and wore T-shirts carrying the black, red and yellow Aboriginal flag. I listened to Bob Marley and the Aboriginal rock-reggae band No Fixed Address, finding defiance in their lyrics of the horror and torment of the white man's world. This was a new identity; I didn't have to hide away to fit in.

We were hungry for knowledge, there were hundreds of questions we wanted answered; we were fired by outrage. I turned also to the writings of Aboriginal poet and activist, Kevin Gilbert. He was related to me, one of our people, a Wiradjuri man. Reading his books filled me with anger. He spoke of the 'shared fact of persecution ... the enormity of white racial injustice ... the cement that binds all blacks in unity'. Australia still struggles with this so-called 'black armband history' but this new narrative would fortify my identity. It became the scaffold for my rebuilt pride, the one I had felt was robbed from me as a child.

Now at university, absorbing ideas and reading these new interpretations of our history, I inevitably became more hardened. I fashioned an identity that opposed Australia. I grew to hate the white blood in me, and all it represented. I mentioned it once to my uncle – my dad's brother – who said his wife (my aunty) would be sorry to hear me say that. He was right – even if I couldn't see it then. My aunty had loved and married an Aboriginal man and raised children proud of their heritage. We could always meet and love white people for who they were. White people themselves were not the problem, the problem was a system built on white privilege.

Still, I delighted in small acts of protest. I can't deny the times I have taken pleasure in seeing Australia's colours lowered on the sporting field. I cheered on the All Blacks or Springboks. I relished the imperious arrogance of West Indian batsman Viv Richards, broad shouldered and fearsomely black, dispatching white Aussie bowlers to all ends of the cricket field. I have even cheered England under the Union Jack flag, anything to extract some revenge, to see Australia – white Australia – vanquished.

All of this is true. Yet I am Australian, not West Indian or South African or Indian or Pakistani. I am an Australian, forged and carved out of our history. I have the blood of black and white in my veins. My fight with history is a battle within myself.

My family is shackled to its past. Australians can consign history to a bygone era. Indigenous people are now told to do the same. We are told to let it go. But our history is a living thing. It is physical. It is noses and mouths and faces. It is written on our bodies.

It is there in the physical scars of people like my father. It is there in the mental scars you often cannot see. These scars are measured in numbers that show indigenous men between twenty-five and thirty are four times more likely to kill themselves than their fellow Australians.

This is the history I feel every time I hold my mother. I feel it every time I think of the future of my children. It is a direct connection to an Irish Catholic convict and a man born before white people had ever arrived here. It is my name and it is my face. In every way I am connected directly to the bloody birth of this country.

PART THREE

'This is your land,' my father would say.

As a boy my family would drive through the town of Canowindra in central western New South Wales. There were shop fronts carrying our name: Grant. There were gates and fences with that same name. We would pass the property of Merriganowry – the word itself felt easy on my tongue. It was as if I'd been born to it and in a sense I was. This was where my father's grandfather was born. As my father said, this was our place.

And so it begins, away back in time before time was even counted here. The rhythms of life were laid down in lore and law and marked in ceremony. Here my ancestor was born on a river his people called the Belabula. His name was Wongamar. He grew up in a time before white people had come to his land. The spiritual and mythical world of the Wiradjuri people was strong. Like all boys, he would be guided into manhood by the people we called the

Walamirra. They came in his dreams to connect him to his land and his forebears.

These were the old men. My people say they are gifted with the power of flight and illusion. They live in a place where time, distance and space dissolve. From here they can see the future. When they came to Wongamar they could have told him of a future he would never have imagined.

My story begins too, in another place: County Tipperary, Ireland in 1810. This was a time of terror and the Grants of Moyne were farmers under the tyranny of English landlords. Gilbert Maher – even for this time – was among the most despised and vindictive of them all. John Grant was seventeen; he was a Catholic, an outlawed religion bound by curfew. With his brother Jeremiah John he rose up against the tyrants. They burned James Shea's house to the ground. He had leased land from Gilbert Maher and had been warned. Jeremiah had tried to kill another man – Gleeson, Maher's agent – and was on the run.

Mary was John and Jeremiah's sister and she turned on them. She was sleeping with Gilbert Maher's son and informed on her brothers. In a book written about Jeremiah Grant, Mary's mind was described as being 'depraved by passion'. Soon John and Jeremiah were in prison and Mary – rejected by the landlord's son – was by now racked with guilt. With her mother, she lured the younger Maher back to her hut and beat in his brains with a rock. They would all hang – all the Grants – but John. This is another one of those moments where fate intervenes and gives birth to an entirely new history. John Grant would be sent to New South Wales and bring his story and his name. It is the name I still carry.

My story is born on the banks of the Belabula and in the hard dirt of Moyne. Two men: Wongamar and John, born into different worlds. But those worlds would soon collide and new families would be formed and torn apart – one white, one black – one family would become Australians and the other outcasts in this same Australia. One family would claim an inheritance that remains today. The other – my family – would see shattered their claim to thousands of years of tradition.

I am what remains. I am a man whose personal journey threads through a story of a new nation formed on an ancient land. My blood, the blood of Moyne and the Belabula. White and black: two worlds that even within me, bend to each other but still can't quite touch.

* * *

John Grant, convict, was brought here and founded a dynasty. He came on a ship called *Providence*. He was a man in chains, hounded by tyranny, banished from the soil of Tipperary never to look on the faces of his brother, sister and mother again. He died the wealthiest Irish Catholic in the colonies.

There is a photo of him. He is maybe forty years old. He is lean and tough, a stern man with an angular face. It is a face that I can't help think resembles a scar. His hair is swept back across his forehead, long and greying. His cheekbones are high and sharp and his nose bent and obviously once-broken. His eyes are narrow and hooded. As I stare into them I see emptiness. His jaw is square and strong and his lips full but pursed. I look for something of me in him, a trace of my ancestry. If anything it is in his eyes, eyes that have absorbed the harshness of the world.

I catch a glimpse of him in another image. This one was taken not long before his death. In the black and white photograph he is with his daughter Julia. He is a prosperous man now. He wears a long coat and hat and is seated in a horse-drawn buggy with a blanket across his knees. He appears like a white slave-owner from antebellum America. He does remind me, with his grey hair and beard and proud bearing, of the commander of the Confederate Army General Robert E. Lee. Perhaps the similarity is not so fanciful. For like the great landholders of the American south, John Grant built his wealth on the suffering of black people. The man who raised his musket to the British landlords now counted himself among them in a new land where he was freed of the chains of his history.

Images of my black family are more elusive. The bones of their bodies feed this rich soil but their names have been mostly erased. Search the official records and we are absent save for acts of charity. By 1833 our family name was written in the Colonial Secretary's reports: mission blankets and rations handed to Tommy Grant, Jeremy Grant. There are other names, but they are not so readily found. These are the names hidden in a shadow world. They lie buried in a potter's field. The register of unmarked graves spills onto the pages of official Grant history. It unlocks secrets long past hidden, long forgotten.

Here, the bodies of dead Aborigines – my family – are given names. Bertha Grant: dead in 1889 just five weeks old. Her father: William Grant – my great-grandfather. There is his sister Selina Glass: dead 1898; and her mother: Mary Anne Grant. There is another entry for Caroline Goolagong: dead 1899, twenty-six years old. Her father was John Coe, her mother listed as Elizabeth Grant (aborigine) [sic]. On and on, name after name filling in the missing spaces in my family tree.

These were the bedraggled and beaten survivors of conflict. They were spared from the gun, poisoned waterholes, arsenic-laced flour, smallpox and venereal disease. They were the sons and daughters of people who had never looked on a white man. Now the predictability of knowledge honed and passed down over thousands of years was replaced with a more tenuous existence. They lived between the grace and charity of some and the brutality of others who would hunt them down like vermin.

This is the history untold in my childhood. A reading of frontier accounts of meeting the Aborigines is replete with casual accounts of utter barbarity. Diaries record food left out to lure the blacks who were then gunned down; hunting parties formed to drive black men, women and children over cliffs to their deaths. The slow certainty of expected extinction was captured by Mrs. Catherine Langloh Parker who looked upon the Euahlayi nation of western New South Wales and lamented:

> As time went on the colour of the blacks seemed to grow paler and paler, until at last only the white faces of the Wundah (spirits of the dead) and white devils were to be seen, as if it should mean that some day no more blacks should be on this earth.

On a property outside Bathurst in New South Wales in an empty field nestled between gentle hills is a plaque that reads:

THE RESTING PLACE OF WINDRADENE *[sic]*, ALIAS 'SATURDAY.'

LAST CHIEF OF THE ABORIGINALS.

FIRST A TERROR, BUT LATER A FRIEND TO THE SETTLERS.

DIED OF WOUND RECEIVED IN A TRIBAL ENCOUNTER, 1835.

'A TRUE PATRIOT.'

This grave is lovingly tended by a family who date their arrival here to the time of Windradyne. In this time blood was spilled, black and white. They fought until they made their peace. Today – it seems to me – that peace still hangs uneasily over this place. I love coming here in the autumn when the golden afternoon light bathes the tips of green trees.

Out here the land feels eternal and still. Time folds into itself and history isn't history at all. It is not something past – it is present. I can stand here now and feel its pull, just as the breeze blows through the rocks as it did then. One day, I would wish nothing more than to be laid to rest here myself buried in the soil of my ancestors, resting alongside Windradyne.

William Henry Suttor was a child of the Australian frontier. His father, William senior, came west after the crossing of the Blue Mountains. He claimed the land that still carries the name 'Brucedale' today. This is the land where Windradyne is buried. William Henry left behind a chronicle of this time – a small book that still speaks to us today of a darker tale than the popular history of my childhood.

It is called *Australian Stories Retold, and, Sketches of Country Life*. Its casual title is reflected in the matter-of-fact telling of the opening up of what would become modern Australia. It is peopled with characters new to this land, people who still spoke with the Irish and old British accents of their homelands. These were people made hard by a journey from homes they would never see again to a place so foreign and strange.

This strange land: big, wide rivers, animals that appeared to be formed from the crazy cross breeding of multiple species, and people: coal black and mostly naked with languages indecipherable. These people could be identified only as a lost relic of humanity's past. To European eyes they were certainly not anything that could be called civilised.

Suttor's book is written in the poetic prose of the nineteenth century. I lose myself in the rhythm of this writing. The names on its pages are vibrant, like something from a Dickens novel: Prosser and Kilminster and Fagan. There are Aborigines: Ippitha and Tommy Bumbo. There are tales of gold and ghosts and pistols and vengeance. There is news of home: home that is still Britain. Suttor follows Napoleon's ill-fated push into Russia. History being forged on bloody battlefields of Europe: great armies coming together.

In his new home of New South Wales William Henry Suttor also sees bloodshed, describing what in those times was just another massacre. It is so matter-of-fact that it barely seems to matter.

He tells of how a group of terrified blacks took refuge in a hut and were then tied together with equal lengths of rope. The men, women and children were taken to a clearing and executed. Suttor's language – that to me so evokes a sense of place – inspires horror.

> Then he sees one of the frightfullest sights human being ever looked upon. There lay the remains of some twenty-eight human beings, all charred with fire and festering and torn, and partly devoured beyond all possibility of personal identification. The remains of men, women, and children lay there in a hideous, sickening, putrefying mass, and the bright Australian sun shining down upon it all.

It isn't the brutality and casual murder only that is so offensive, it is that this is just so common. It appears so unremarkable.

It is in the accounts of settlers like William Henry Suttor that I can piece together a war – and that's what it was called – that came to define my ancestors. This conflict helped determine our place in the world. We still suffer from its wounds. Suttor's book continues with its languorous yarns about country life. There are cattle musters and bushrangers, the funny side of dealings with the blacks and friendships formed. But then the book is suddenly punctuated by more killing. And Suttor tells of a conflict that came to his father's property. The blacks of the Bathurst plains – my people the Wiradjuri – rose up against the death that was all around them.

As Suttor describes, the Wiradjuri:

> … commenced general depredations, killing solitary shepherds, destroying large numbers of sheep, and they actually got possession of seven stand of arms and some ammunition. In the course of a short time, hostile contests having taken place, several Aborigines, as well as Europeans, were killed.

Martial law was soon declared. Suttor writes 'the blacks were shot down without any respect'. Aborigines were lured to huts with food under the pretence of negotiation and then killed. Amid this violence a leader made his name known and feared. The whites called him Saturday. The Wiradjuri knew him as Windradyne.

Years ago I walked the property where Windradyne now lies with a descendant of the original Suttor family. John Suttor was the great-grandnephew of William Henry whose book shines such a light into our darker history. We wandered in that mid-afternoon autumn light that always feels holy to me. It is a spiritual time for a spiritual place. The rocks we passed had the formation of old ritual sites – initiation grounds for Aboriginal boys to transition to men. John was wiry and grey. He had spent a lifetime on this land and he spoke of it as sacred. To him this was a battlefield as meaningful and definitive to this place as Lone Pine is to Gallipoli.

As we walked he drew on his family's history handed down through the generations. In a peaceful valley nestled among trees leading up a gently sloping hill was a deserted dilapidated hut; it was right there, John said, that Windradyne confronted the original settler William Suttor senior.

The old white man met the black leader and his band at the door. He spoke Wiradjuri fluently and convinced Windradyne and his men that he brought no harm or threat. They clearly accepted what Suttor had to say. The Wiradjuri men left and headed for a nearby property. There, they slaughtered three farmhands. Today the area is known as Murdering Hut.

This was the start of a three-year cycle of attack and reprisal. A price was placed on Windradyne's head: 500 acres of land for whomever would bring him in. There were other killings. More Wiradjuri people took up arms and followed Windradyne's lead. Farms were raided and torched, stock was slaughtered. The whites launched their raids and formed gangs to ride out and kill as many blacks as they could find.

The *Sydney Gazette* described this as a war of extermination. There were more raids, more deaths. Food was laced with arsenic and left out for the Aborigines. More settlers were attacked. But victory for the Wiradjuri was never a possibility. With their numbers depleted, Windradyne led the remnants on a march to Parramatta to meet Governor Brisbane. Adding an improbable sense of theatre, the black leader – so despised and hunted – wore a straw hat with the word 'peace' written on the brim.

The Suttor family has its stories; and we have ours. These stories meet here in a land where white and black still live alongside each other. We are together but positioned on opposite sides of this chasm of history. But we can see the humanity in each other – the descendant of settlers and the descendant of the Wiradjuri. He belongs as I do. His family's blood runs deep here and the name Suttor has earned its place. It is in meetings like this that I can find a real hope for what our country might be.

* * *

My family's name – Grant – emerged from this bloody tangle of history. It was a name written on mission blankets and on title deeds. John Grant, once an Irish convict, was now emancipated and pardoned. The one condition: he must never return to Ireland. He would never again see Moyne. He would never see the graves of his executed family.

Instead, he built a new life here. He followed the explorers crossing the Blue Mountains. He established his first holdings in the mountain village of Hartley. Next he claimed a vast property at what is now the town of Canowindra. He named it Merriganowry. It was a Wiradjuri name – the people whose land he had taken.

By 1828 the Wiradjuri uprising at Bathurst had been subdued. In the census of that year, John Grant was listed as having 4000 acres near Bathurst. He ran 5000 sheep. The man who had once been in chains now counted fifty-six convicts working for him.

Tragedy continued to stalk John Grant. In Australia his first wife died. She was only in her thirties and John was left with three young children. It would be seven years before he would remarry, this time to the young daughter of a Protestant free settler. What a transformation from outlaw Catholic rebel to landed gentry married into respectability. John Grant and his new wife Elizabeth had nine children.

Tracing my family's direct connection to the convict turned squatter is more difficult. It is lost in a time when my people were literally written out of history and excluded from official records. But certainly by the 1830s blacks appeared carrying the Grant name. My search of unmarked graves revealed a shadow world where my black ancestors had the same names as their white half-brothers and -sisters: Elizabeth, Hugh, Mary, William, Selina. These black Grants often went to work as domestic servants for their own white siblings.

Out of the haze of this frontier Australia, one name emerges. William Hugh Grant, an Aboriginal boy born in 1856 and raised on Merriganowry. He later married a white woman from nearby Cowra. His marriage certificate lists his father as John Grant, squatter. As in all families, there is argument and conjecture. There are competing stories and myth that shroud his birth and parentage in mystery. This one document – the marriage certificate – provides the only evidence.

Where official records may fail, I have my imagination to try to fill in the gaps. It isn't hard to see a property with a white master and his growing children, surrounded by blacks still living on what they would consider their land. Like a scene from the slave plantations of the American south, the blacks worked as farmhands and cooks and cleaners for their new white landlords.

Here William Hugh – Bill as he became known – grew into manhood. One part of him followed the traditions of his people, guided by his black grandfather into the rituals of manhood. Another part of him, though, perhaps looked at the old boss, the now grey-haired and frail Irishman, and felt an equal pull of family. The old man too may have looked fondly on the boy. He was black but fair skinned enough to imagine the white in him would lift him above the seemingly doomed fate of his darker brothers and sisters. An eventual white wife would open the door to a world in which Bill's descendants would lose all trace of their blackness. This is a story lifted straight out of the pages of Australian history and later written in government policy that would try to make us more like white people.

Bill Grant lived well into his eighties, his life spanning the young nation's own growth from federation to war and depression. He died on the cusp of the next war. He did not fulfil any supposed or hoped-for white destiny. His first marriage ended and he married again, this time to a woman of his own people. Bill Grant had three more children. One of them, Cecil William Henry, was my grandfather.

I have only one photograph of Bill Grant – my great-grandfather. He was an old man when it was taken. Its faded black and white image is difficult to see clearly. He is dressed in a long coat and a hat. He appears strong and lean. He has a thick moustache. His Aboriginal heritage is notable in his dark skin and broad nose but there is an unmistakable trace of European too. He is standing next to what remains of a scarred Aboriginal ceremonial tree. The markings on these trees tell our story and are said to be the soul of our people.

Bill Grant's life itself traces the contours of the story of this country. He was born onto the fringes of a people facing a predicted extinction and raised on a property owned by a former white convict he believed to be his father. He ended his days on a mission set up to ease the misery of the remnants of the Wiradjuri; now homeless and adrift in his land. I visited the site of that mission, now long gone. I found a place of ghosts. All that remained were the stumps of vanished mission houses. In a small book listing the names of the people of Bulgandramine mission I found something else, something that makes sense of the life I have lived. It connects me to my love of words and stories. In this book there is a listing for Bill Grant. Next to it is one word: storyteller.

* * *

On the banks of the Belubula the worlds of Moyne and Merriganowry came together in a meeting of two men. John Grant's journey had taken him across the sea to his new land more wide and open than any he could have imagined as a boy, where he found riches and raised a vast family. Wongamar had been born to this river before any white man had crossed.

His name has been carried down through the generations of my family. Wongamar speaks to me of an earlier time when my people mastered their own destiny. My uncle – my father's brother – carried his name. Somewhere, sometime, my two ancestors came together. The circumstances are buried with the men themselves but there is a physical reminder of that place and time. John Grant had a brass breastplate made for Wongamar inscribed: 'King of the Meriganourie'.

These were commonly handed out during the early days of the Australian frontier to acknowledge local leaders. It would often encourage greater cooperation between black and white. Today some may see these artifacts as mocking or cynical. I can understand that. But I also like to think in my family's case this might have been a moment of genuine affection. I will never truly know, but that breastplate is a physical connection – a marker of a new family that was created here out of a convict from Ireland and a man of the Wiradjuri.

PART FOUR

As the frontier passed, my people were not fading away. We had become the 'Aboriginal problem' and now there was a solution. It was a great Australian prophecy, written in law and given a name: Assimilation. As the policy stated: '... the destiny of the natives of aboriginal *[sic]* origin, but not of the full blood, lies in their ultimate absorption by the people of the Commonwealth ...'

Absorption: think about that word. To us it meant that we would lose all traces of our culture and our heritage. It meant that we would lose our families. In *The Destruction of Aboriginal Society*, writer and teacher Charles Rowley describes the policy as one where my people were 'regarded by governments as a phenomenon of transition rather than as an end in himself'. Its aim, he said, was to ensure Aboriginal people 'disappeared altogether into a white community with no coloured enclave'.

I have a photo that tells me so much more than any policy document. It is of a group of Aboriginal girls outside a welfare home in the New South Wales town of Cootamundra. They are all staring blankly. Barely anyone smiles. Standing in the middle, one of the smallest girls is my great aunt.

Aunty Eunice was my grandfather's sister. Her life was ruled by the *Aborigines Protection Act* of 1909. It restricted her movements and had as one of its stated aims, the removal of so-called half-caste children from Aboriginal reserves. In a twenty-year period from 1912 more than 1500 children were taken from their parents. Aunty Eunice was one of them.

She is listed simply as case number 658. Her file records her name, age and place of birth. It says she was recommended for removal by the manager of the Aboriginal station in Cowra. She was taken from her parents to the girls' home and then to work as a servant for wealthy squatter families. So many of these children were forever lost to their families. They would never see home again. Aunty Eunice did make it back, but life was never kind. She died still young, leaving orphaned children.

Australia had us trapped in its pervasive whiteness. My grandparents, my parents, on down the line to me. All of us were measured for our potential to become white. Here was a supposedly humane answer to the destruction and extermination of the early decades of settlement. In the earlier era of so-called protection we were rounded up from our traditional lands and put on missions to be 'christianised' and 'civilised'. These missions paid little heed to kinship and the boundaries of our nations and fell too quickly into neglect and often into violence.

We were the 'half-castes' who had stubbornly refused to disappear. A black American writer W.E.B. Du Bois once stated that the great problem of the twentieth century was the problem of the colour line. And here we were.

We baffled governments who tried to place us on a trajectory towards whiteness. They failed to see we were human. We kept our culture alive and our people together. We married each other and reinforced our visible identities. Sometimes we married white people and in their own way they too became black. Not just to us, also to a white world so puzzled at why they would choose us that they would have them punished for it.

* * *

My grandmother – my mother's mother – crossed that line and in so many ways never came back. The law took a dim view of this love. In some parts of the country, it was illegal for a white man to marry or even have sex with a black woman. It must have been completely unthinkable to our lawmakers that a white woman would deign to love a black man. They never counted on my grandmother.

Ivy Sutton was as white as a white person can be. She had blue eyes and blonde hair. Her background was German on her father's side. She was raised in small town Australia, Coonabarabran, nestled against the Warrumbungle Ranges in New South Wales. A more conventional woman may have grown up, finished school, married a local farmer and become the matriarch of a white clan. Not Ivy.

There was nothing conventional or predictable about my grandmother. To be honest, to some she must have appeared a little crazy: wonderfully crazy. She wouldn't have even considered race, let alone racial divisions. She would have thrown her nose in the air and set herself above it all like the glamorous 1930s Hollywood movie star she thought herself to be. She named one of her daughters Marilyn, but the real Marilyn Monroe had nothing on Ivy.

When she was fourteen Ivy was thrown out of home. Her mother – I am told a mean-spirited, hard-nosed and frankly mad woman – sent her to help one of her aunts who had recently had a baby. After some months Ivy returned home to find the door locked and her mother packed up and moved in with another man.

Ivy was stranded with nowhere to turn. For a moment she thought she'd escape into the convent and become a nun. There was a problem: Ivy had barely spent a day in church in her life. She presented herself to the convent but was packed off to a welfare home.

When Ivy was released from the home, she was again destitute. Her mother – now remarried with another child – didn't want her. But Ivy was never deterred. She remembered a good-looking, dark curly-haired Aboriginal man who lived down by the river in a tent. He'd whistle at her when she passed. So Ivy moved in that night and stayed more than twenty years, raising nine children and burying three more.

I am stunned today at the audacity of my grandmother. I am reminded of that time in our history; a time when my people were not fully recognised as citizens. There were laws that determined where Aboriginal people could live. We were locked out of swimming pools and pubs and confined to roped sections of movie theatres where we still had to stand for the national anthem. Here was a white woman – who called herself a white Aborigine – shunned by her mother and now outcast from her society and on the wrong side of the law.

My grandmother told me how the police would stop her in the street as she pushed her babies in a pram. They would upturn everything searching for alcohol, accusing her of running grog to the blacks. They obviously didn't know her well. Ivy had never touched a drop of alcohol in her life. It didn't stop with police harassment; the local hospital refused to take her when she was giving birth to her first child. Ivy had her baby in the back of a car as she was driven to a nearby town in the hope of a better reception.

Ivy never married my grandfather. Legal formalities had no real place in their lives, and anyway, she said, she was never sure when she would leave him. It was a joke, but sadly one that would become reality.

I can't know the inner workings of their relationship. Whatever personal failings there were could not have been eased by crippling poverty and rejection. There was the constant heavy-handed intrusion of police, the prying eyes of welfare officers and threatened removal of children. Theirs was a life of dirt-floored tin humpies, skinned rabbits, card games that lasted for days, hungry children and in the middle of it all, a pale-skinned, blue-eyed woman surrounded by black faces.

It broke Ivy. She fled one day, ran off, met another man, a white man, and was married within a matter of weeks. She would tell my mother that she had lost her mind, and realised only too late that she couldn't turn back. But Ivy never forgot the curly-haired boy who whistled at her from his tent. She never stopped loving him and he loved her until his dying day.

She is gone now, my nan. But I could never forget her. She called me her 'Guggy boy'. As a baby I couldn't say Daddy. It came out Guggy, and that's who I became. I used to love to tease her. I would stretch my neck and she'd scold me, warning I would stay like that. She used to tell everyone one day I would be Prime Minister. She never forgot my birthday. My nan did the same for all her grandchildren, each year sending a card in the mail with coins tied in a knotted handkerchief.

Ivy: bright red lipstick, steel wool yellow hair and always talking. She was like a machine gun. One sentence would run into another. Often she was barely coherent, just thoughts tumbling over and over each other. She thought she was Patsy Cline. She needed no prompting to burst into song.

Ivy, who would sometimes still run off with my pa: the man with the tent. They would relive that great love, that forbidden love, the love that couldn't survive death and poverty and the police and the history that separated them.

* * *

Keith Cameron was born under a tree near a place called Baan Baa between Narrabri and Gunnedah in inland northern New South Wales. Keith's mother was Jessie Sutherland, a Kamilaroi woman. She died when her son was only a baby. But she was from a big Aboriginal family who made a home for young Keith.

I remember him now as the most important person in my young life. My grandfather lived with us off and on throughout my childhood. We had no idea then that he had been born with only one functioning lung. He had worked on the railroads, ridden a bike for hours at a time and was a talented tennis player. But it had a damaging effect; he was often short of breath and would constantly cough up phlegm. My pa had a habit of grinding his teeth as he perched on the steps or verandah of whatever house we called home at the time. I'd sit with him as he circled his picks from the racing form guide, 'Three-Way Turf Talk' on the radio beside him.

He was a very funny man. He could go to a pub without a cent and come home drunk from free drinks as he entertained people for hours with his endless jokes. He did love a drink; he could go many months sober, but eventually he would break out. My mother told me once how he had been up all night swapping beers with my father, their voices growing louder as the night grew later. Finally Mum had had enough, she burst into the room, grabbed the last of the beer and smashed the bottles on the floor. My grandfather looked up in dismay but without missing a beat dropped to his knees to lick up the remnants.

Pa would send me out running through the streets if the mailman was late with his pension cheque. He'd demand to know where the postman was. He was always telling me how white people only cared that their guts were full. Cheque finally in hand, he'd take me to the local Greek café for an ice cream before heading for the pub. I'd wait up in bed for him; for the crash against the wall as he stumbled, drunk in the dark. He'd always be singing, usually Engelbert Humperdinck's 'Please Release Me'. I would leave my bed, careful not to wake my brothers sleeping with me. I would help Pa inside. Then I would comb the grass looking for any money he'd spilled on the ground. I would hold Pa's loose change for a few days until he was broke again and I'd surprise him with this small forgotten windfall.

Keith was itinerant. He moved from home to home between his children scattered across New South Wales and his cousin Neville's house in Baradine on the edge of the Pilliga scrub. All he owned he held inside an old battered brown suitcase, his port he called it. He carried his clothes, and his dog-eared copies of Zane Grey cowboy novels. He also carried an old photo. It was of a beautiful, vivacious, irresistible, irrepressible, blonde woman who moved into his tent.

* * *

Betty Cameron bound the worlds of Ivy and Keith. Along with her brothers and sisters she stood in the gulf of our history. She lived straddling the fault lines of her blood and her country. She was one of those pale faces that tempted the authorities eager to imagine they could turn black kids white.

The welfare's in town!

The welfare's in town!

How fast the word gets around.

… that just won't do, we hear them say.

Maybe we'll send the kid away.

She turned the world of her childhood into verse. She passed the stories on to me, her son.

My mother's poems tell of pain and pride; of joy and just simply getting by. But her poems also served as a warning to me. This is why I was so terrified when the welfare men came to my school, because they had come for her too. She said they would throw back the blanketed doors of the tin shacks my mother and her family fashioned into a home. They would enter at will to check on the kids.

But the Aboriginal families anticipated these visits. They hatched a plan. They would fill the powdered milk tins with flour. They'd gather up what meat or vegetables they had and share it among themselves. They would fill otherwise empty shelves. As the welfare left, children would gather the possessions and run them to the next humpy. On and on they would repeat the same charade, until the government men had left. But my mum knew, as all Aboriginal families knew, that the welfare would be back and they wouldn't always leave alone and families would never be the same again. They wouldn't even be complete families again.

My mother is a keeper of stories. She would dole them out as part of the bargain of my childhood. I would scratch her head or rub her feet in exchange for another of her tales. She lives in a world touching the supernatural. Ghosts hovered around her childhood. She told me about the man on the white horse who haunted the showground she'd pass through to get home each night. There was the old lady in the hospital; the small, crippled man in the wheelchair who would vanish in one time and place to reappear days later in another.

Spirits are not strange to us. They are not relegated to the realm of fantasy. The believers and seers are not mocked. We like being scared. But there's another reason: we live closely with death. Death stalks our people. It can take us young, sometimes before we have even had a chance at life. Death comes with a warning, animals transformed into prophets of doom.

The willy wagtail was a harbinger of sorrow for my mother's people and when she was only a girl it came to rest outside her home. My mother told me how her mother, my grandmother Ivy, tried to chase it away. But the small black and white bird returned. It sang a song of the dead. It sang a song for my mother's little brother Neville. The night before he had been rushed to a hospital with a fever and now the news that he was gone brought no surprise. My grandparents placed his tiny ten-month-old body into a box. In it they placed his tiny white booties. My mother had picked some wildflowers and she buried them with her brother.

My grandparents eventually buried three children. That was the price of poverty where kids' survival was a roulette wheel. A tin humpy and the makeshift graves of lost lives, this was sacred ground to my mother's family. But they had no hold over their lives or their land.

One day the police came with a gun and a bulldozer. A developer had bought the land and one by one the blacks were being cleared out. My grandfather had nowhere to go and perhaps was just tired of running. He'd buried his children here. He'd made a home here. His woman was white, his kids were light skinned, he worked, he fed his kids and they went to school. He was told this is what Australia wanted from him. He wouldn't move. The police put a gun to his head and in front of his family, my pa dropped to his knees and the bulldozer levelled his little humpy.

* * *

I can see my grandfather Keith, now nearly forty years dead, I can see him spending hours just sitting, looking into the distance. He loved feeling the warmth of the sun on his face. I can see that little tin humpy long gone. His home now was just a suitcase and wherever he happened to be. Gone too was Ivy. She lived in a caravan down by the river, near her daughter Lorraine. I can see my pa when he'd pass close by and just sit at a window for hours staring at the river.

* * *

My mother has the soul of a poet. As Wilfred Owen, the English writer and soldier, said, all the poet can do today is warn. So my mother couches her warnings in memory. She remembers her brothers and sisters and her mother and father and another time when they huddled against the world. And she remembers little things. These things that never leave her and can call her home.

> Speckled fruit mum used to buy.
> Rabbits we used to fry.
> Broken biscuits made you cry.
> I often think of days gone by.

We could do nothing to stop government officials invading our privacy. Our homes and our bodies could be violated at will. My mother told me how her father was arrested out of his own bed because police claimed he had been drinking. He wasn't taken to the police cell; instead he was tied like a dog to a tree and left there. His children passed by him the following day as he sweltered in the sun.

Stories of police brutality were common. My father faced it first hand as a young man on the streets of inner-city Sydney. He learned what it was to be a black man in Australia at the boot of a policeman.

I read about this in an old court case. Another Aboriginal man, Kenny Brindle, had seen the police kicking my father. He screamed at them to stop. He said there was no need to kick him. But this was a time of violence. Dad has told me about how often he and his mates were harassed and beaten by the police. Perhaps it explains why he took such time to prepare me for this world. It was why he spent those hours teaching me how to throw a punch and defend myself.

Stan Grant – my dad – was like so many other young black men of his time. He was cheeky; he was out with his mates drinking; and that was enough to put him under a cop's boot. It wasn't the first time and he wasn't the first, and still it happens. Black men go into police custody and don't come out.

* * *

My father could well have been one of those awful statistics. He could have joined that tragic list of black men whose deaths have never been properly explained.

As a young reporter I wrote stories about these cases. The numbers had jumped alarmingly. There were calls for a national inquiry. Finally a royal commission was announced. Witnesses would come forward to lay bare a national shame. They would tell of young lives cut short, of unrealised potential.

One of those cases has always stayed with me. I spent time with this young man's mother and father and saw the terrible anguish that his family had to endure. It all began one afternoon in a small country town – a town like so many I was raised in.

'Come on, Eddie Murray, we want you. Come on, Eddie Murray, we want you.'

It was broad daylight; two o'clock in the afternoon in Wee Waa in the New South Wales cotton belt, a place that is hard, hot and isolated. These towns were bred on segregation. These are the towns that Aboriginal writer Kevin Gilbert knew too well. He travelled these towns and he found people like himself. These were people, he said, with a 'sidelong averted gaze ... exaggerated attempts at dignity ... overdone affected bravado'. These Aborigines, he said, know they don't belong. They know they're not accepted. They are what he called 'outcasts and misfits in their own country'.

The cops from this hard hot town came for Eddie Murray. They taunted him with that song, 'Come on, Eddie Murray ... Come on, Eddie Murray.' Witnesses heard it and they saw the police take Eddie Murray. They never saw him alive again. Eddie was drunk, they said, hopelessly drunk. Under the law of the day the police could detain him 'for his own safety'. Detain him, not arrest him. They could have taken him home instead they took him to a cell. In an hour Eddie Murray would be hanging from a prison-issue grey blanket.

He was no longer Eddie Murray the cheeky son. He was no longer Eddie Murray the footballer. In death, he no longer even had a name. He was a black body in a police cell. He was a body marked with the tag 'belonging to police.'

Those police who came for Eddie Murray said he had killed himself. He was drunk, his blood alcohol reading would have put him six times over the legal driving limit. In this state, it is said, he tore a prison blanket into strips. They said he made a noose, threaded it through the cell bars and hung himself. The coroner did not believe it. He found there was 'no evidence on which to be satisfied the deceased committed suicide'.

The coroner said part of the police evidence was 'unreliable'. But he still found no one to blame. Eddie Murray, he said, died '... by his own hand or the hands of a person or persons unknown'. Exactly who, the coroner would not say. He left the matter open and a family with only questions.

Eddie Murray lies in an unmarked grave. It is now three decades later. There have been inquiries. The police investigated themselves. His case helped establish the Royal Commission into Aboriginal Deaths in Custody. His body was exhumed and a new injury detected. It was found that he had a crushed sternum and it had occurred before he died. No one has explained exactly how Eddie Murray died, only that the police did not do it.

Still there are calls for a truth that makes more sense than a drunken hanging and smashed sternum. Eddie's mother and father died still searching for something they could believe. They could never square this death with their cheeky, tough boy. They could never see their son as that lifeless body tagged with the words 'belonging to police'. Lawyers still argue for new investigations. Eddie's sister Anna still sees her brother. He is forever that body lying in a morgue. Her brother will forever be twenty-one. He will forever be the boy who taught her to fish.

* * *

There are so many others: black people assailed, beaten and dead. Others, taking their own lives, in the dark hours of prison lock-down. A roll call of tragedy: ninety-nine names. There were ninety-nine deaths in nine years in the decade before the 1987. All of them were investigated by the royal commission, which made 339 recommendations. And still the deaths continue. Indigenous people are locked up in numbers that should horrify us. My people are fewer than three per cent of the Australian population yet we are a quarter of the prison population. Among kids it is worse, half of those in juvenile detention are indigenous. Jails breed depression and suicide. One in five indigenous male prisoners try to kill themselves. Among women it is nearly one in three.

I interviewed one Australian criminologist who said that the rates of imprisonment are 'unbelievable'. But we believe it. To us it is all too real. The same criminologist told me that we are locked up for crimes that would see other Australians walk free. He said it isn't because there is rampant crime in black communities. Indigenous people murder and rape at half the rate of the general population and commit drug crime, about eight times less. But once locked up indigenous people begin a spiral of reoffending and jail. Over and over people are trapped in a cycle of violence, drugs and alcohol, mental illness, sexual abuse, unemployment and abject poverty.

To criminologists these are statistics; to us they are mothers, fathers, uncles and aunties, brothers and sisters, sons and daughters. These numbers have names and faces. They have names like Stan Grant, my name and the name of my father who could so easily have been one of these statistics.

* * *

My father has worn his life on his body. I remember it as a boy, a body of tattoo and muscle. He has a stab wound on his shoulder from an angry Greek café owner in Sydney. He has a lump the size of a golf ball in his foot. It is a steel plate, the legacy of his football career with the Newtown Jets. He told me once he'd been poisoned and had nearly every bone in his body broken at some time. The tips of three fingers are missing. It is the price of a life in the sawmills to put food on our table. These are the scars and battle wounds you can see. But there are others from a lifetime of living black against a sharp white background.

My father refused to be defined by the harshness of this world. He is a man who still buys flowers for my mother. He is a man softened now by the god of second chances. In his twilight years he found his voice. He rediscovered a way to speak to this country that had silenced him.

By the middle of the twentieth century my father's language was dying. It had largely vanished, wiped out by missionaries and government officers who forbade it. My father caught the last utterings of Wiradjuri. His grandfather was among the final keepers of the traditions and ceremonies and he would speak in the bush to my father, educating him in the way he and his father before him had been educated. But once he made the mistake of calling to his grandson in front of the whites. Downtown Griffith was no place for this. The police arrested him and he was jailed. When he came out he refused to speak his language again.

But the seed his grandfather had planted now flourished. John Rudder was a linguist from the Australian National University. He wanted to save the Wiradjuri language and approached my father. John asked my father to work with him and together they composed the first Wiradjuri language dictionary. They established learning centres and travelled the state teaching. Then they taught others to teach. Now the Wiradjuri language, once on the verge of being extinct, is spoken and learned in schools and universities and prisons. Our people are proud and my father feels worthy. The struggle of his life has been worth it.

* * *

A couple of years ago I stood with my father as he was honoured with a Doctor of Letters from Charles Sturt University. I stood beside him with my mother, my sister, and our families. My father had outlived the police brutality of his youth. He had stayed one step ahead of the welfare men. He had worked and fed his family. Now he was here being acknowledged for saving a language his own grandfather had been jailed for speaking.

I wonder now about the lives that could have been. I wonder about Eddie Murray and the ninety-nine others.

I wonder about those who continue to die in custody. I wonder how we can lock up entire generations of people. Since the royal commission's recommendations the incarceration rate of indigenous people has increased by 100 per cent. It is worse today than ever.

* * *

Dad had been raised among his people in western New South Wales. His mother was from a big Aboriginal family, her father one of the last initiated Wiradjuri men. Her mother was Nanny Cot, who I spoke about earlier. If you trace my family tree you can fill Aboriginal families from one end of New South Wales to the other: Johnson, Naden, Simpson, Glass, Coe, Ingram, Goolagong, Merritt, Gray: just some of the names on my father's side.

These are the families that had been formed out of the frontier – Wiradjuri families with the names of white settlers. We emerged from the missions scattered around the state. Our parents and grandparents worked picking fruit or as farmhands for local farmers – working land that was once theirs for the descendants of people who had taken it from us.

The migrant story is often hailed as the great example of Australian opportunity; how people can come here from foreign lands carrying nothing and build successful lives.

They are praised for their hard work and sacrifice. Well, my people worked hard and sacrificed too but were still too often denied the Australian dream. We are told now to stop playing the victim; these people were never victims. When Australia asked them to step up they did, even if it meant leaving their families to fight in a war for a country that didn't even count them as citizens.

* * *

In 1939, Dad's father – my grandfather – enlisted to fight in World War II. Cecil William Henry Grant carried the name of his Irish convict ancestor. His father was born out of the conflict on the frontier – a direct link to that time of dispossession. My grandfather was brought up on the missions between Cowra and Dubbo. He was one of many children, his mother – a Wiradjuri woman – had several kids when she met his father, old Bill Grant, and he too had an earlier family. Cecil had well over a dozen siblings. His mother died when he was only young and his father was an old man when he was born. My grandfather's sister was taken away by the welfare agency and Cecil spent much of his young life on the road before he met and married my grandmother, Josie Johnson.

Now he found himself in Egypt in the trenches of Tobruk. He would recall how one step was the difference between living and dying; one step, and he'd survive while the Digger beside him takes a bullet in the head. Another step forward into the darkness under a hail of fire, machine guns blazing and mortar shells landing all around him. He threaded his way through the landmines and booby traps. On and on through the night to nowhere really, but each step meant he was still alive.

The 9th Division spread across a two-brigade front. Their objective was miles in the distance, now they had to take ground, hold it, wait for the next brigade to fill the breach and move forward; on and on. A mess of flashes and explosions and confusion and more men silhouetted against a gun-lit night sky.

More men falling, mates; mates far from home, far from being blackfellas and white men. Mates, now facing a common enemy. All of them, now just wanting to get back home. At home they would fall back into line, take up positions once again across their old battlefield. Back home the Australian frontier separated them, but here in Egypt they were just a tangle of limbs. Men, all blood and spit and tears.

* * *

My grandfather came back from a war fought for this country with the sound of Tobruk still in his head. He came back with a photo, Diggers lean and tired. Their shirts are undone. They are squatting and looking directly into the lens, not at each other. These Diggers are Australians and they are white. But the one in the middle is unmistakably different. He is black and unlike his mates he is not an Australian. He is not counted as a citizen. But he is there and he is fighting just like them.

The Egyptians thought he was one of them. They told him he belonged there. But he came home to where he was really from, where he really belonged. When he came back he was told his sacrifice counted for little. He was wearing his uniform and tried to board a train. The conductor told him he was back home now and had to walk. The Egyptians thought he wasn't Australian. Now one of his countrymen too was telling him he wasn't Australian.

* * *

I am fast approaching the age at which my grandfather died. It seems so young but in my memories of him he was never young. He is the straight-backed man in the white shirt. He is the man of the church. In God he found somewhere to rest his demons and put aside the pain of war and prejudice. He heard in the words of the gospels a deliverance and equality that eluded him elsewhere. This religion was born in the missions. It was a religion of refuge, a haven from the onslaught of the frontier.

This was the religion of the slaves in plantation America. It focused on the suffering Christ on the cross, Jesus asking why he was forsaken. Here lives would be played out in a drama of salvation and backsliding and forgiveness. This was the religion of the Aborigines Inland Mission whose monthly reports beseeched its followers to spread the word of God 'O'er lands that still in heathen darkness lie.'

But this religion gave order and structure and meaning and hope to the lives of people like my grandfather. He became a so-called 'native worker' and preached in the missions that were his home. He preached sermons of obedience and reason. He campaigned for justice with his mates like Jack Patten and William Ferguson in 'Aborigines' Progressive Associations' who pleaded for their people to 'live in the modern age, as modern citizens'.

My grandfather moved his family onto the fringes of white society, off the missions. He found work picking fruit. He sent his children to the local school. When they came home and told of taunts and abuse he told them that they were as good as any white person and to be proud of who they were. He became the first Aborigine to work on the local Griffith council.

I struggle to recall him properly; my memories are hazy. But if I allow my mind to clear there is a touch that I know is real. I can feel his arms, strong and cradling me. I can see myself reaching up to tip his hat from his head. I can feel my lips on his dark skin; I can feel my fingers poking into his broad nostrils and my cheeks nuzzling against his jowly face.

If he were here I would ask him why he fought for this country. Why would he leave his wife and children to wear the uniform and fight under the flag of a country that denied him even the right to be counted among them? There are so many questions.

But I have the answer of his example. He was a Wiradjuri man and when whites came to our land we fought them and then he fought alongside them because Wiradjuri people fight and we get up. He had one more fight not long before he died. After many years he finally decided to march on Australia's sacred day, Anzac Day. He placed his medals on his chest and walked the main street of Griffith with his old comrades.

The local police sergeant watched him. Here was a black face in a parade of white Diggers. The cop watched my grandfather walk to the pub with his Digger mates. The sergeant blocked the doorway and told him he couldn't enter. My grandfather had stopped drinking years earlier, but he pushed through and ordered a beer. His mates –

white men he'd fought alongside – surrounded him and defied the policeman. In that moment my grandfather was an Australian. His God said he was equal and he was still proudly black.

PART FIVE

My family is like so many other Aboriginal families. What has happened to us has happened to all. We have felt the brutality of Australia. We have had our land – our inheritance – stolen. Our language was banned. Our children have been taken away. We have been herded onto missions. We have been forced onto the margins of society. We have lived in tin humpies and tents. We have been powerless before the state. Welfare officers and police have invaded our lives at will. We have been told to become like white people, yet when white people loved us and had children with us they too were punished.

It would be so easy to surrender to this oppression. The weight of history in Australia suffocates us. I have said it before but it demands repeating – our history leaves its mark on our bodies and our souls. I have seen people crushed by whiteness. I have seen people deny who they are – lie to their own children – to escape the fate of blackness. They prefer to disappear into a world that has never wanted them anyway.

It is so easy to walk through this country and be blind to it all. I am still surprised – although by now I should not be – at how often people tell me they just didn't know. Yet it is there right in front of us. The reminders are everywhere. It is written into our landscape. It is there at Waterloo Creek known also as Slaughterhouse Creek where perhaps as many as 100 people were killed. It is there at Myall Creek where twenty-eight people died. It is there at Poison Waterholes Creek and Murdering Island. There is the Rufus River Massacre, the Evans Head Massacre and the Nyngan Massacre.

Why do we not know what happened at Murdering Gully or the Campaspe Plains or Halls Creek or Fitzroy Crossing or Margaret River? Rivers, mountains, ranges, plains and deserts have become graveyards for my people. Australians pass by these places oblivious to what has happened in their own country. They are oblivious to us as well. We live alongside them. We have worked with them and for them. We have fought in wars we were told would make us free.

The Australian anthropologist W.E.H. Stanner, writing in the 1960s, spoke of a great history of indifference. Stanner had spent decades living alongside Aboriginal people. He studied our societies and recorded our histories.

He sought to place the suffering he saw all around him with the timeline of Australia's progress.

Stanner's Boyer Lectures are still considered a high watermark in our efforts to grapple with the impact of colonisation on my people. He spoke of our powerlessness, our homelessness, our dependence and poverty. These things, he said, produce a syndrome of inertia, non-responsiveness and withdrawal. He saw an emerging great reckoning of this Australian silence. His words ring as true today as they did then:

> What may have begun as a simple forgetting
> of other people's views turned under habit and
> over time into something of a cult of forgetfulness
> practised on a national scale.

As much as we look away we cannot truly ignore each other.

I remember former Prime Minister Paul Keating telling the truth about what happened in our country. It was in Redfern in Sydney – sometimes called the spiritual home of Aboriginal Australia – and I was there on stage with him. Thursday 10 December 1992 was International Human Rights Day, as Keating strode to the podium. Not too many years before I was delivering office mail and photocopying, now I was introducing the Prime Minister to speak to my people.

I had spent several years reporting on this bruising, eloquent, stylish political figure. I had always been fascinated by politics. My interest was sharpened in the tumultuous days of the early 1970s, watching the rise of militant black activists. Like many in Australia at the time, I can remember where I was when I heard the Whitlam government had been dismissed. I was sitting in a bus stop waiting to go home from school, overhearing the news on a radio. I went home and watched the ABC news that night as Gough delivered his immortal lines on the steps of Parliament House.

Now I was working here, watching up close as Keating helped transform this country's economy – floating the dollar, opening up the financial system, creating more competition and productivity. He had steered us through – and sometimes directly into – troubled seas. The recession he told us we had to have, sent interest rates soaring, drove businesses to the wall and cost thousands of Australian jobs. Reform, however, was long overdue and the changes then built a platform for the decades of growth to follow.

Keating was a man of great ambition and he was in a hurry. I recall him striding the corridors of the Canberra Press Gallery, a posse of minders in tow. It is fair to say it was a sight that would inspire a collective gasp. Certainly to a young reporter like me, it could be intimidating. We began one interview with Keating leaning back and tempting me to 'go on son, do your best'. He was a combative and often entertaining interviewee. He could be extraordinarily dismissive too. He would greet reporters waiting for his arrival outside the parliamentary doors on an icy winter's morning with a backhanded wave and the words 'disappear, disappear'. Eventually he had ropes erected to keep us even further away.

The man fated to become Prime Minister – a man who left school in his mid-teens and entered parliament in his twenties – eventually claimed the job, toppling his one-time friend and ally Bob Hawke. As Prime Minister, Keating raised his gaze from just the economy, he wanted to transform our notion of ourselves. He spoke of our need to embrace Asia, he championed the arts, he wanted to change the flag, remove the Queen and supplant Gallipoli with Kokoda. This day he wanted us to reckon with our past.

Keating gave me a cheeky wink as I introduced him and stepped aside. I stood just behind him alongside Sol Bellear, a black man who had fought – often physically – for the rights of his people. The crowd continued to chatter, the murmur competing with Keating's own voice. Slowly though, they began to hush. This would not be just any speech. These were words we had not heard from a Prime Minister. Sol and I looked at each other, trying to take in what we were hearing.

'We took the traditional lands and smashed the traditional way of life,' he said. 'We brought the disease, the alcohol; we committed the murders; we took the children from their mothers; we practised discrimination and exclusion, it was our ignorance and our prejudice.' Yes, this was our story. This was the story not told in our classrooms. This was what my parents had told me, what I had seen as a young boy. This was the source of the fear that lived in us all. With each word the crowd clapped and cheered, it was a collective release, a relief that now our history was being told.

Keating challenged the country to do better. A prosperous and harmonious society, he said, surely can find solutions to the problems that beset the first Australians. Keating reminded us that it begins with recognising the first injustice, the original act of dispossession. It was we – white Australians – he said, who did that dispossessing.

More than twenty years have passed since that Redfern speech and the work remains undone. Keating spoke recently again, this time at Sydney's Opera House and lamented that a great country cannot be truly great until we have resolved the original grievance.

Terra nullius – an empty land. This legal doctrine underpinned our dispossession. It rendered lawful what might otherwise have been theft. As a people we had no rights, indeed were legally invisible. This belief persisted for two centuries until a man from an island in the Torres

Strait exposed the lie of this nation's settlement. I had read about Eddie Mabo in law journals and scant reporting of his case in local Queensland media. He had challenged the courts to recognise his existing continuing traditional title to his land on Mer – or as it was known, Murray Island. Time and again he had failed. Time and again he appealed. Now it was listed for a final hearing in the High Court – there would be no more appeal. *Terra nullius* would stand or fall on the argument of this man from Murray Island and his legal team.

It is a cliché that journalism is a front row seat to history. It is also often true. This was a potentially historic moment. On the morning news conference call I told my editors of a story that could overturn the very foundation of this country. There was scepticism, almost disbelief. Really? This case is that important? Eddie Mabo was a name unknown, his case wrapped up in legal technicality. At its heart though was a simple question: was the British claim on this land based on a lie?

It took several years after that first day, that first story I reported for ABC news, for the court to strike down *Terra nullius*. Eddie Mabo fought until his death. The struggle took its toll on his health. He passed away from cancer on 21 January 1992, aged only fifty-five. Five months later the High Court delivered its final judgment. To the justices themselves who made this ruling, this was about who we were as a nation. Australians could no longer cling to the fiction that this land was empty, that the original people had no rights. Everything came from this: the murders, the missions, the stolen children – all of it. Now in the highest court in the land, our law was saying this was wrong. Two of the judges wrote that Australia had 'a national legacy of unutterable shame'.

* * *

Journalism has been my salvation. It has taken me around the globe. I have seen the worst of the world and met people who have inspired me. In a career now spanning more than three decades I have reported from more than seventy countries, I have lived on three continents and have seen the world turned on its axis. I was in South Africa as the racist policy of apartheid was dismantled and a black man – Nelson Mandela – who had been locked away for a quarter of a century became President. I covered the troubles in Northern Ireland – the centuries-old battle between Catholics and Protestants. This was a story that reached back into my family's history. My forebear – John Grant – was banished to Australia for his part in the Irish rebellion trying to overthrow the British.

War in Iraq and Afghanistan, terrorism in Pakistan, the intractable Israeli–Palestinian dispute, the rise of China, the secret world of North Korea – I have seen it all. It all began with a fire in the suburbs of Canberra and my news director throwing me the keys to the car. I had been hired as a cadet reporter only weeks before. Tony Bartlett was the boss of the local Macquarie Radio station and had decided to take a chance on me. My job was to write news copy, record interviews, present news bulletins, fetch lunches and clean the cars. It was a steep learning curve.

I could barely believe that just a few short years earlier I was drifting, delivering mail at the Institute of Aboriginal Studies. Marcia Langton had lit a fire under me. Other Aboriginal people like historian Gordon Briscoe opened up a world of ideas. Now I was on my way as a reporter, and this was my first test.

I had fifteen minutes before news time at the top of the hour. I had to get as close to the fire as possible and file a report on what I saw. Street after street was blocked, police waving cars – including mine – away. The clock was ticking and I was growing desperate. Tony Bartlett called me on the two-way radio to check on my progress, I couldn't tell him I was failing. I assured him everything was fine and then hoped it would be. The news bulletin was only minutes away when I took one more turn. I had seen a hill and decided this was my last chance to gain a vantage point. It worked. I topped the rise as the news theme was playing, the news reader crossed to me and I was able to describe the scene below: fire raging through trees, smoke billowing into the sky, people hosing down their houses.

I moved quickly through the early years of my career, from radio to television with the ABC. I worked in Canberra as a political reporter alongside some of the best journalists in the country. It was a competitive place, but I also found colleagues were generous with their time and support for me.

I made a conscious decision that I would not be the 'indigenous reporter'. I railed against this straightjacket. I had seen other black people embark on careers – lawyers, doctors – only to be marginalised; the box ticked Aboriginal. This way was career death. It is one of the reasons we are still largely absent on our TV screens, why we don't have an indigenous person on the bench of the High Court, why we don't run our top companies, or head surgical teams in our hospitals. Until recently we had never had one of our people on the front bench of either major political party – almost every other ethnic group in our society has been represented but us.

I wanted to be seen as a professional in my own right. I wanted to cover any story I was interested in: politics, sport or international affairs. For journalism to be effective, first it must be good. Stories need to be well told, built around compelling characters and images. If I was to have any impact or be able to tell the stories of my own people I wanted first to be a credible reporter.

I have had opportunities I could not have dreamed of – certainly not when I was being asked to leave high school in Griffith when I was fifteen years old. I have worked for almost every television network in Australia. I have hosted prime time programs seen by millions of people. There have been missteps – programs I am less proud of, especially in the often tawdry world of ratings-driven commercial TV. For all the highlights, though, nothing comes close to the years I spent with CNN. There is my career before CNN and after, and I was never again the same person.

PART SIX

I am alone in a land far from my own. Out here there are no fenced horizons, there is only a vast openness. If I look for distractions I find none. There is just silence and sand. There is not even a tree to measure my distance. I can walk and walk, on and on, with no purpose, no destination. There are no straight lines here. The landscape rises and dips but each mound is indistinguishable from another.

This is a stark beauty. In the pre-dawn light the huge sky is like a child's painting smeared with colour and filling the whole page. But it lacks the drama of my country. Where I'm from there would be waterholes and hills and ghost gums and rocks settled into place over eternity.

In my country the air would fill with the scent of eucalyptus and, depending on the time of year, wattle and wheat that stings my nose. But here there seems to be no smell. For all its strangeness though, I don't feel a stranger here. This too is ancient land and the people here like me are people of the soil. This is not a place of transit; people haven't wandered its breadth in search of the next place to call home.

The people here are built close to their earth. Their skin is dark and battered by the wind until its texture is like leather. Their eyes are narrowed, set in broad, squat faces. Their bodies are powerful with torsos longer than limbs. They are wrestlers, these people. And horsemen. Their horses are like themselves, muscled and sturdy and relentless. The horse once carried these people to an empire greater than the world had ever seen. This is a land of animal spirits and totems. This is a land of wolves. This is a land of nomads. This is the land of Genghis Khan.

On the steppes of Mongolia, the winter temperatures can plummet to minus 40 degrees Celsius. In the darkest coldest months of the year 2000 thousands of head of livestock were wiped out in a single blizzard. It was the biggest freeze in thirty years. Ulaanbaatar has been called the coldest capital city on earth.

I came here first in the depths of winter. My eyelids turned to ice and I could touch the bridge of my nose and feel it crack inside. I could walk just a few metres and feel my body convulse. The blasts of air driving into me like spikes. The sky was grey and polluted from the choking smoke of coal. As the vast open land to the north seemed to me to have no smell, the city burned with a stench of heavy industry.

I came back as the winter turned to spring but by then my own darkness had fallen. I didn't need refuge from the howling winds of the Mongolian plains, I was battered by the storms of a history I thought I'd left far behind. The past months had been sleepless and my hands had begun to tremble. At night I'd feel a heavy weight pushing down on my chest and my breathing had turned shallow. I would gasp constantly, trying to catch my next breath. I was worried that the one after would not come.

I had grown obsessed with time. I was driven to account for every second, always trying to beat the clock. I would mark every day in advance, plotting what I would do and where I needed to be. It would start at 6 a.m. when my local gym in Beijing would open.

I had measured the short distance from my house. I would go out of the gate, down the street, around the corner, into the building and up the stairs to the gym's front doors. I would arrive exactly on the stroke of 6 a.m. and then plan my workout to finish in precisely one hour, then go to the café, buy my morning coffee and be home no later than 7:30. My coffee had to be boiling hot and even then when I arrived back at my house I would put in the microwave for thirty seconds. I would eat, shower and be ready to leave by 8 a.m. for the drive to my bureau's office.

One second lost was a day ruined for me. To be a minute late for the gym was enough to light a fuse of anxiety that would surely explode sometime that day. To counter that possibility I would set my alarm even earlier. Even then still I would lie in bed watching the minutes tick by before rising to my feet to make that perfectly calibrated journey.

In time that too wasn't enough. Now I would sneak in as the cleaners left from the night before. The gym wasn't even open. Soon I discovered where the cleaners left the keys and I would open the doors myself. I would turn the lights on and be training before anyone else arrived.

So, here I am watching a clock ticking in the darkness. Three o'clock then three-thirty then four and five. Day after day I push back morning until I am wide awake by 2 a.m. Soon I am barely sleeping. I fight exhaustion all night. My eyes may close for a moment; maybe ten minutes until I wake again and stare at the ceiling. I check my emails and watch the minutes tick by.

Hour after hour this goes on: me heaving and gasping, and my wife waking throughout the night and trying to calm me. Sometimes she will gently rub the point between my eyes and I drift away but not for long. At other times I wait for her to come to bed, filling the room with my own toxic nervous energy then deliberately provoking an argument over any trivial issue I can find, anything to create drama and fuel me with enough anger to drive me through the restless night.

I don't know when exactly my mania began. I was never a deep sleeper and my mind was always turning. But lately it had gone into overdrive. By now I had spent years on the road as a correspondent for the international news network CNN. I was the senior reporter based in Beijing and covering all of north Asia. I had also spent time in war zones for the network; travelling in and out of countries like Afghanistan, Pakistan and Iraq. Before being posted to China for a second stint I had been assigned to the Middle East, stationed at our bureau in Abu Dhabi.

Wherever I was posted I drove myself to the point of collapse only to push through and test new barriers of endurance. I became renowned for my punishing work schedule. I would make myself available around the clock. For a twenty-four-hour global network there is no night; the news churns on and on.

I would ride every change of shift and every time zone speaking to television producers in Atlanta, New York, London, Hong Kong. If they needed me on air I would be there. I demanded the same from my cameramen and field crew. We'd rest sometimes between live reports. We would go down for two to three hours but then wake and begin the cycle all over again.

While others slept I would wake after an hour or so and then read or plan my day or do some exercise. Near our bureau in Islamabad there was an oval and running track.

I would go there and run lap after lap. I would clock up to ten kilometres then come back, shower and eat and rouse my team for another day.

I would immerse myself in the news, politics and history of whatever country I was covering. I consumed books and magazines and newspapers at a furious rate. I have always had good recall of facts and I had no problem speaking endlessly on air, taking any question no matter how detailed or obscure and weaving a coherent and hopefully insightful response. But there was another motivation: a riveting fear of being exposed, of looking foolish or out of my depth or being unmasked as a fraud. That propelled me more than anything.

The road to Mongolia and my moment of reckoning was long. I can see now it began on the back roads of country New South Wales and it wound its way through the freeways of Europe, the narrow mountain passes of Pakistan, the gunbarrel highway linking Amman and Baghdad, and the corrugated hilltop tracks of southern China.

This journey took me into the lives of people in pain and misery. I was drawn to these stories. It wasn't the machinery of war or politics that inspired me; it was the common humanity of those whose existence was determined by forces bigger than themselves. I wanted to know how they found the courage to face another day when all certainty had been stolen from their lives.

I remember them all so clearly. There was a man in Soweto, South Africa, a black man who had been kicked down by the boot of a racist political system. Now in the dawn of a new Mandela age of freedom he was welcoming me and a television crew of two white Afrikaaners into his home. He shared with us his meal and his story and he called me his brother.

He was not unlike another man I met in Baghdad. He was not an Iraqi, he was a Palestinian whose family had fled with the creation of the state of Israel. He had found a new home in Iraq, and lived a quiet life of family and work, each day knitting together family and friends and the rhythm of a life trying to stay free of politics and the heavy hand of the dictator Saddam Hussein. War had come now to his new home. Again he confronted uncertainty and fear. But always thoughts of the home he had fled were never far away. He carried with him a glass jar containing dirt from Jenin in Palestine, and with it a dream that he may one day touch that earth again.

I reported stories of sacrifice and endurance and the love of family. I met a man once who carried his son for forty miles down a mountain in Pakistan. His boy had a broken leg; another of his sons was dead. With him were his wife and their other remaining child. All they had was what they carried. His home had been demolished in an earthquake that tore apart entire hillsides and buried towns. They came to a relief camp where they were given a tent and some meagre supplies. I saw them from the window of our car, just a light in the distance, a small fire where a woman cooked a meal for her family.

The light drew me – it happens like this sometimes as a reporter; something speaks to me, compels me to listen. When we approached they sat around the fire and told me of their struggle. The youngest boy told me all he wanted was to go to school again. His mother broke down as she relived the trauma of the son left buried under the rubble of their demolished house. I saw the man again the next day. He was standing with other men. They had gathered in the local town square waiting and hoping that they would be chosen for whatever work was going, whatever they could do to earn some money to care for their families.

There are so many faces, so many stories. I met terrorists, men with improbably gentle voices who told me how they programmed others to kill. I was taken on a ride into a closeted world that existed right under the noses of security and officials. We left Pakistan's capital Islamabad for a town a little over an hour's drive away. We had brokered this meeting for weeks. Through an intermediary we had won the confidence of the local Taliban commanders. They had something they wanted to say and they would say it to us.

The man I would meet was among the most wanted figures in Pakistan and Afghanistan. He was one of the right hands of the supreme Taliban commander, Mullah Mohammed Omar. This man had helped orchestrate a siege at the Red Mosque in Islamabad that ended in a bloody shoot-out. He had survived and fled over the border to Afghanistan, through the badlands of the tribal areas of northwest Pakistan where authority came from kinship and the gun. Now he had crept back within touching distance of the capital he had turned into a bloodbath.

We were heading into territory controlled by the militants; Pakistan security ended at the town limits. We were instructed to drive to a crossroad, slow down and flash our lights. Do not stop, we were told. Two cars pulled out: one in front, one behind. We were escorted down a series of roads before coming to a stop next to a small nondescript house beside an open field. We had taken the precaution of notifying our head office; in turn they had informed our security company, who would monitor our every move.

We weren't alone. Pakistan has been called the most dangerous country on earth. It is nuclear armed, bristling with guns, and is the breeding ground for global terrorism. We had a former British Special Forces soldier in our vehicle, he travelled with us on all assignments and kept in regular contact with his people back in the UK. If we were late or missed a call-in CNN would notify Pakistani authorities. The risk of course is that by that stage it could be too late. Reporters had been kidnapped and killed before this.

The man who greeted us was strikingly tall. He towered over us and we were all around six feet. He had a full beard and was dressed entirely in white including his turban. He would not shake our hands or even so much as meet our eyes. We were infidels – non-Muslims – and he wanted no part of us.

Throughout our interview he averted his gaze and we were under strict orders to film only the back of his head. As a fugitive he needed anonymity and as a cleric showing his image was forbidden. Two armed men stood by my cameraman to ensure he complied.

He had agreed to our interview only because Mullah Omar – his leader – had dispatched him to Pakistan to deliver a message to the local Taliban. Omar had issued a new code of conduct for militants and was concerned that the Pakistani Taliban was violating these ethics. The local Taliban were particularly brutal. They had seized one part of the country – the Swat Valley – where, as a message to others, they used to hang beheaded corpses in the middle of the town of Mingora, an area known as 'slaughter square'.

I travelled to Mingora soon after. The Pakistani military had successfully driven out the Taliban. I had befriended the head of the army's northern forces, General Nadeem Ahmed, who personally flew us in his own helicopter. As we swept over the beautiful valley – described as the Switzerland of Pakistan – he pointed out militant bases and we could clearly see men moving around below us. It was an uncomfortable ride.

The General had taken us to meet a group of boys who had been rescued from the Taliban. They had been kidnapped and reprogrammed into suicide bombers. They were farm boys mostly, once happy and outgoing we were told. Now they were shells. The light had gone from their eyes. When we were introduced to them they looked only at the floor. We sickened them. To them, we were westerners or worse Americans, the very people they had been trained to kill.

After being snatched from the fields, these boys were deprived of sleep, sexually and physically abused and forced all the while to endlessly recite the Qur'an. Their heads were filled with hate. Eventually they would become so dehumanised they would strap explosives to themselves and target western forces. Sifting through this human wreckage, this terrible waste, psychologists were hoping one day to rescue their minds as their bodies had been saved and reunite them with their families.

I saw the end result of this brainwashing. Too many times I was called out to suicide bombings from the Middle East to Pakistan and Afghanistan. I recall one attack in Beersheba in Israel. Palestinian fighters had targeted two buses, entering and simultaneously detonating their vests. The death toll was staggering; a scene of twisted metal and shattered glass. Ambulances ferried the wounded and collected the dead.

In such scenes it is difficult to relay the horror, the seemingly senseless barbarity. Yes, there is history here and politics but that is for another time, this is about families and loss. Amid all the carnage one image conveyed more than any words I could speak or write, there among the shards of glass was a packet of chocolate teddy bear biscuits not long opened and still mostly full, and on it the bloody hand print of a tiny child.

I covered the so-called war on terror on and off for a decade. I am reminded that a war that began with an attack by Islamic extremists on the heart and soul of America on 11 September 2001 has claimed the lives of more Muslims than any other group. In the years since 2001 more than 30,000 Pakistanis have died in terrorist-related incidents. War in Iraq and Afghanistan, civil war in Syria and broader conflicts in the Middle East, Asia and Africa send the death toll into millions and many, many more have been left destitute and homeless.

I recall another suicide bombing outside a police cadet school near Peshawar, Pakistan. Two men had ridden motorbikes into a graduation parade and exploded their bombs. When we arrived soon after, the bikes were left twisted on the ground, cars were upturned and the windows blown out. There were pools of blood on the ground and the air smelt of explosives and burning flesh.

As is Muslim custom, the families of the dead were collecting body parts and bits of bone and skin, some of which had lodged into shrapnel holes in the walls. They would carefully place the remains of their loved ones into plastic bags ready for traditional burial before sundown. Inside the burnt-out wreckage of one car I saw a blood-smeared bookmarker with a Qur'anic verse praying for a safe journey.

I tell you this because all the while I was ticking too. I plunged into these dark worlds, propelled forward by a sense of duty and responsibility to my employer but more than that a sense of loyalty to these people who were trapped in a hell on earth. Death waited at every dawn and those who escaped were only given a reprieve until the next day or the one after that. The survivors were left to mourn and rebuild and pray; these people let me in, they shared their stories and their grief. Why? Because telling a story helps, but they also wanted the world to know they were human and they were suffering and they weren't so unlike all the rest of us.

I didn't seek gun battles and soldiers. I sought the small lives. My job was to lift their stories out of what can otherwise be an endless, heartless tally of numbers. I owe it to them to tell you who they are. There was the young boy I saw in a refugee camp. His family had fled the war in Afghanistan. Not this war, the war of the 1980s when what was then the Soviet army invaded. War has ravaged Afghanistan for centuries. This boy had never seen his homeland; his entire life was in the confines of a miserable camp in Pakistan. This country would never accept him and the land of his parents was lost to him.

I saw him leaning against a tin and tarpaulin shack balancing his withered leg with a homemade crutch; in his hand was a plastic bag and inside that, more plastic bags. I approached and through an interpreter asked about his life. 'What are your dreams?' I asked. What a stupid question. He looked at me as if I'd asked if he'd touched the moon. I asked instead what he wanted to do with his life. He looked down at the bags and said simply, 'This,' and shook them. He sold the bags each day, standing by the roadside. He would gather as many as he could find and hope that someone would stop.

Why would he do it? Why not just surrender? This is what drove me to work day after day, to push myself beyond sleep. Where do people get this pride and dignity? From where does this spirit spring? But of course, I knew the answer. I had seen the same sacrifice and determination all of my life, in the faces of my family.

It is the countries with the deepest history that entranced me. China, Pakistan, Afghanistan, North Korea, these countries that have fought for their survival. China wears the scars of Japanese invasion and occupation; Pakistan is locked in existential struggle with India, born after the brutality of partition; Afghanistan is the graveyard of empires, fighting wars of attrition from the armies of Alexander the Great to the might of the Americans; and North Korea remains in a state of war, with the Korean Peninsula split in two.

I measured my own people's plight with the struggles of these people far away. The Chinese speak of a hundred years of humiliation; how foreign powers made them servants in their own land. They would repeat a vow to eat a thousand years of bitterness, to endure any sacrifice and hardship. I devoured the history of the country: the war against Japan; the civil war between the Nationalist forces of Chiang Kai-shek and the Communist Red Army led by a peasant general Mao Zedong.

I met the last survivors of the Long March, women who took up weapons alongside men. I stood in the home of Mao in the hills of Yan'an, where he sought refuge, regrouped his fighters and then swept to victory. I remember a photo of Mao and his comrade and deputy Zhou Enlai; this is not the rotund Chairman of the People's Republic the world would become familiar with. This was a thin, haggard and hardened young rebel. The two men lean against Mao's hut in their military greens, their eyes drawn and tired but undeniably defiant.

Anyone who knows anything of Chinese history could not be lulled into a false romanticism. These were times of great brutality and Mao's policies would inflict enormous suffering on his own people. The Great Leap Forward would end in great famine and tens of millions of deaths. Yet Mao's image hangs large like an emperor over the Forbidden City and his body rests in a mausoleum in Tiananmen Square. People still come in thousands to pay respects. Mao's photo hangs in nearly every rural home, and in the cities even the young still revere him as the father of their country.

I saw it all as the contradiction inherent in any nation's history. Jefferson held slaves; Churchill sent thousands to their deaths at Gallipoli; yet both are giants in the stories of the United States and Great Britain. In Australia Henry Parkes, the Father of Federation, campaigned to ban Chinese from the goldfields. Racism and bloodshed don't disqualify leaders from our mythology. To the Chinese, Mao – whatever his failings – is the link between their country's humiliation and its renewed greatness.

In Afghanistan and Pakistan I met tribal men who had studied the warfare of Mao. They had formed insurgencies, understood there could be strength in apparent weakness, inspired loyalty and fear in local populations and over the decades had helped banish the Soviets and now were intent on driving out the Americans.

There were many warlords and rival guerrilla armies, but the Taliban had emerged most powerful. Their name means 'the scholars'. They came out of the Soviet war; often orphaned children raised and schooled in strict madrassas – Islamic schools. They had a sense of drama. They carried the Qur'an and the gun; they wore black turbans and black eye shadow.

The Taliban first won favour with women. They made them feel safe, vowing to free them from rape and violence. They targeted corrupt and brutal provincial rulers, overthrowing them and hanging them for all to see. They imposed sharia law, music was forbidden, men ordered to grow beards.

Then the women they promised to liberate were locked out of schools and locked indoors. They gave safe haven to Arab mujahideen, among them a rich Saudi exile named Osama Bin Laden who had formed a militant cell he named al-Qaeda – the base. From Afghan soil Bin Laden plotted an attack against the United States that toppled New York's Twin Towers and struck the Pentagon; we know it today by its date 9/11.

I was fascinated by Pakistan and Afghanistan. I could hold the past here in my hands. I walked into a dusty shop in what was known as 'Music Street' in Kabul. There was a time when these stores were banned and the musicians who owned them, beaten or jailed. Now the Taliban had been toppled.

A coalition led by the United States had struck back after 9/11 driving the militants from power and back into the hills. There was noise and joy here again. The smell of bread and kebabs wafted down the street, vendors sold locally made ice cream, and cluttered instrument shops were open again. On a wall I saw a battered guitar, its strings rusted, left behind by a Soviet soldier from another war.

The man at the counter spoke no English but I motioned to get it down and he placed it in my hands. I plucked out a tune, eventually picking the opening chords of Led Zeppelin's 'Stairway to Heaven'. This man then reached for his own traditional instrument – a rubab – a type of short-necked lute and impossibly difficult to play.

Slowly he found a rhythm and we locked in sync. Here we were, two men who could not speak to each other communicating in music – an Afghan who had known little but war and a reporter who had come to tell the story of the Afghan's country and a rusted old Soviet army guitar meeting across time and space. I lived for moments like these.

So much of my job was about our inhumanity, the savagery we inflict on each other. The guitar I held in my hands came to this country with a man who also brought violence. When the Soviet soldier arrived he found a country already tearing itself apart. He probably didn't even want to be here. Some didn't want to go home. They stayed, married Afghan women, had Afghan children. These young Soviet soldiers became Afghans. And now I held a Soviet army guitar and I played with a man who had known nothing but war. Together for a moment we found, in our simple joy, what it means to be human.

Of course, I wasn't just a reporter; I was never just a reporter. The stories I covered were as much about me as the people I reported on. What – I wondered – did these countries tell me about my own? Here were people in their own lands, the lands of their ancestors. Like my people, their homes were invaded. Foreigners across the centuries had brought the gun and law and religion. These people too had been dominated, their land taken, their languages forbidden.

I reported on the horrors of these places: the suffering of poor Chinese left out of their country's new riches; the Afghan and Pakistan civilians killed in bombing raids or slaughtered by militants, their heads severed from their bodies; Koreans separated from their families by the dividing line of the Cold War, some now starving and risking all to flee a regime that controlled their very thoughts.

Didn't my people suffer too? Were we not forced from our homes? Were we not slaughtered? Did some of my people still not live as refugees in their own country? I have always felt that our history has been diminished. It lacked the epic sweep and grandeur of great armies or marauding hordes. We were a small people in a distant land. How many times have I heard that we should forget our history; move on? Yet, it happened to us. Our lives have been as shaped and defined by these forces of change as anyone I met in China or the Middle East.

But there is a difference. These people still had their country, they fought under a flag of their choosing, and they sang their anthems. They had fought each other; they had fought outsiders; but this was a destiny of their making. We resisted invasion too, my people struggled – and struggle still for our rights – but we were overrun, and our fate decided by others. Long-term conflict may never have been a viable option for us and this country has been spared the internecine insurgent warfare of other lands, but the impact on us is no less real.

I grew to understand that conflict doesn't end when the guns stop, that its legacy is passed through the generations. I learned how it casts a shadow and the shadow doesn't recede, and no matter how far we travel from the battleground that shadow hovers still. We know this.

We know that lives lost young and needlessly in war cut deeper and stay with us longer than those who pass in the normal flow of life. These fallen are timeless, we recite odes to them: 'They shall grow not old, as we that are left grow old.' And the survivors of conflict measure themselves forever against those times when they were tested and hold in their hearts forever those who were sacrificed.

So, here I was in Mongolia. On the steppes where Genghis Khan drove his armies and fanned out to conquer the known world; here I fell under the weight of my history. Of course it needn't have happened here, this is just the place I was when I could run no more.

I shouldn't have even been here. The sleeplessness, the obsession with time, the tremble in my hands, the gasping for breath; these were all products of trauma and an aching exhaustion. When an empty milk carton and a two-minute walk to replace it is enough to trigger an explosion of temper there is clearly a deeper problem.

There had been other signs: lately whenever asked to go on assignment I would acquiesce and then privately fly into a rage, hurling clothes around my room. Occasionally I had struck myself hard in the head, or slammed my fist into a wall out of frustration. Sudden loud noises made me jump, and when I did fall asleep my wife said I would lash out and swing my arms, or my legs would kick as though I was furiously running to escape something. Once at work I could function perfectly well, in fact I was even more productive, more prolific. No matter how tired, I could always do another live cross or write another story.

I had resisted speaking to a doctor, insisting I was fine. My wife had tried to coax me, telling me something wasn't right. CNN took the welfare of its staff very seriously. We would be given downtime and there were counsellors to speak to. I'm sure it is common for people under stress to deny there is a problem; certainly that's what I was doing. Finally even I knew this could not go on.

I found comfort and inspiration unexpectedly, in a voice from home. Singer Normie Rowe was being interviewed on a podcast of the ABC Radio program *Conversations*. I listened to his story. He spoke of his own battles after war in Vietnam and his spiral into darkness. I haven't been a soldier and knowing a little of what they face I wouldn't even begin to compare my situation. But Normie's story connected; it was simple and it was gentle and there was no judgment.

I remember clearly the night in my bedroom in Beijing that I spoke by phone to CNN's consulting psychiatrist. He is a man familiar with the trauma of reporters and war and stress. He has written a textbook study of the impact it can have. He listened as I told him of my symptoms and my experiences.

He asked about my sleep patterns, my moods, my work demands. He asked me if I enjoyed anything anymore and it occurred to me I had stopped listening to music. Music is a mainstay of my life but now the CDs gathered dust and my guitar sat propped against a wall. He diagnosed my condition and told me I needed to stop work immediately, take some time out and see a doctor. He was based in Canada and offered to fly me there. But I decided I needed to go back to Australia, back home. First though, I had one last assignment to complete.

My trip to Mongolia was meant to be a little reward. A nice easy trip to a fascinating country; no dead bodies. The President of Mongolia admired my work – yes, it sounds boastful but seriously at CNN the power of the brand and its reach inflates the value of all of our work – and he invited me to his country to travel with him to his ancestral home. We would shoot some picture stories and contribute to CNN's feature programs focusing on a slice of life in exotic locations.

I assured my wife I'd be fine. When I returned I would make plans to take time off. I still hadn't told anyone at work and requested the CNN doctor not divulge anything just yet. I was a little quiet but that wasn't unusual and my crew thought I was just engrossed as always in another book. Maybe there was a clue in the book I was reading, a biography of Syd Barrett, the doomed, crazed genius of Pink Floyd.

On the flight from Beijing to Ulaanbaatar I became anxious. I actually wrote an email to my boss explaining that I was going to resign and move back to Australia. I spoke of how I was feeling and that it was simply time to make a change.

I had broken rule number one: the doctor had told me whatever I did make no decisions while I was under stress. Rule number two: take an immediate rest. Here I was making a life-changing decision and flying to a remote country with my heart beating and my head pounding.

Again, at work I was a model of calm: engaging, interviewing people, laughing, seemingly on top of everything. Then, back in my hotel room I was crying, ringing my wife constantly. My despair would come in waves. At times it was overwhelming. I would feel it like a physical rush, as though it was coursing through my veins. I can't explain why people take their lives but I do know that at those critical moments impulse could easily cloud reason. These attacks would last perhaps only a matter of minutes and then I would settle back into my melancholy.

Two weeks this trip was set down for and each day became more fraught than the last. The President had no idea how I was feeling. We flew high up into the mountains to the village of his birth. His extended family, goat herders and horsemen, nomads still, all gathered to greet us.

We slept in a traditional Ger – tent – and ate wildlife like marmot – a type of large squirrel that live in burrows and are common on the grassy Eurasian steppes. The President would catch and prepare his own and delighted in sharing it with us. We filmed our stories and took long horse treks through the mountains.

The next destination was a great lake on the edge of the Gobi Desert. Again, we pitched tents and locals brought us mare's milk vodka and wild animals to eat. Even in my most anxious moments, trying to balance my work, keeping up appearances and calming my breathing, there were moments of absolute farce.

The President was highly competitive and a strong sportsman. Being from Australia he supposed I was a strong swimmer so he challenged me to a race in the lake. He had his bodyguards measure 100 metres. They positioned themselves at the start, the halfway mark and the finish line.

It was a ludicrous scene. The President of Mongolia, a short – it has to be said – stout man with a round stomach, a mane of jet-black hair swept back from his forehead. He emerged from his tent in a pair of swimming trunks that I have only ever seen favoured by men in North Asia: black and skin tight, running halfway down his thighs. These would flatter no one. He was surrounded by his personal security, similarly decked out. And then there was me in board shorts wondering what in hell I was doing there.

My body was beyond exhaustion, I had a head full of death and misery and to be honest I just wanted to throw up. The President decided to claim a fifty metre head start and put me on the back mark. Now I was faced with either disgracing myself and shaming my country's honour or actually beating the President and embarrassing him in front of his staff. In the end I came close enough to maintain my dignity but not enough to lower his. We were both winners. And for a moment I could shake my head and laugh at the absurdity of it all.

I still wasn't sleeping but I'd become expert in pretending. To avoid the President's next challenge or being fed the heart of a rodent I would close my eyes tightly and hope it was enough to be left alone. I think I may have even pretended to snore for added effect. I would listen as my crew and the leader of the Mongolian people settled for the night and then in the depths of darkness I would creep out of the tent and walk.

I would wander for hours until the tents were a dot in the distance. Walking was all I could do to quiet my mind. I was flooded with despair and a gut-churning sense of loss. I ached and the world just seemed so pointless.

The day before, we had been filming from a helicopter and seen wolves roaming the sand dunes. But now I didn't even consider that I could have been torn limb from limb. All I wanted to do was walk, just for the sake of keeping moving and staying awake. Then at dawn I would make my way back to the camp and slide into bed to pretend that I'd never been away at all.

Through it all I would call my wife, making little sense, just babbling and crying. She was deeply worried. She had contacted my boss who had tried to call but I wouldn't answer. One of my closest friends in Australia was alerted and he phoned me. We spoke and he comforted me and tried to make sense of my muddled mind. If I could just get through this, I thought, I would go home and get help.

On the final night we were booked into a glamorous resort outside the capital. These were tents for kings; enormous with huge beds and deep baths. Finally I was alone and I could soak in the water and wash away any pain. This was what I had seen as a boy: my father sore from work and collapsing into hot water his eyes closed and for that moment, still.

These were the thoughts that crowded my mind. It wasn't the misery of war and poverty and oppression that I'd been reporting on for years. I had absorbed all of that. I had empathised and shared the pain of others. I had tried as best I could to do justice to their plight and find the words that could not just tell their stories but move people a world away to care.

It weighed heavily on me and my crazy work ethic had hollowed me out. These people had their struggles; but these wounds now were mine. This was a story I had not told. Reporting on the suffering of others had unlocked a door to my own soul.

By now I would sob uncontrollably and over and over again just scream: why? Why had they done this to us? I was on the phone again to my wife and she listened as I rambled about my mother and my father and my grandfather. They were so good I said, they were so beautiful and Australia had kicked them down.

I remember saying we didn't deserve this. All the anger, all the hurt and confusion were tumbling out of me. I didn't know anymore where the war in Afghanistan or the terrorism in Pakistan ended and my world began.

All the people, all the faces – the children dead in earthquakes, the corpses I'd seen piled high and set alight after the tsunami in Sri Lanka, the woman I'd met who fled North Korea and was now terrified of being discovered and sent back to face certain death – all of them merged with mine and the faces of my family.

All the horror of the world, all the misery and injustice, all of it collapsed into my own history; history I had thought I had left well behind.

I am reserved and private. Even among family I hold my feelings close. I told myself I shouldn't be feeling like this. I felt guilty about those people I had met and reported on and then left to their fate. Among my people I was one of the lucky ones. I had a loving family, a fascinating career and I was financially comfortable. Others were more deserving of this pain. But now I see none of us is immune. This is not just about me, about my own struggle; it speaks to something much deeper among my people.

My doctor diagnosed me with acute depression, an illness that afflicts one-third of indigenous people over the age of fifteen. We are twice as likely to suffer as other Australians. My doctor was very clear: I had a disease and that disease can kill. For Aboriginal people again the rate is alarming; we are nearly three times more likely to commit suicide. I was a time bomb and like so many of my people, the fuse had been lit in childhood.

There is no doubt my state of mind was affected by exposure to the ugliness of the world: years of reporting war, death and misery. But that accumulated trauma awakened a long dormant malaise. Everything was torn open. All that sleeplessness, the roiling anger, the deep sadness: it didn't come from Pakistan or Afghanistan or China. It was Australia that had brought me so low. Australia was all I could think of and it flooded me with despair.

We speak of a community of fate, a shared inevitable destiny. This may appear to be a forlorn fatalism, a grim acceptance that we are bound to an inescapable misery. This nihilism can breed its own destruction. It can become a self-fulfilling prophecy. To the more comfortable among us this fatalism is defeatist. We can imagine that an education and a job can break this cycle. But explain that to a boy with scabies and sniffing a tin can of petrol tied around his neck, or a woman in prison whose son is also locked up. Explain that to a girl in her room trying to read a book and block out the screams and shouting outside her window.

These are lives that are real. Sadly they are far more real for my people than the world in which I now live. These are the people who inhabit the headlines. They are the victims and perpetrators of rapes and bashings; they push drugs that they too are hooked on and spread disease that they die from. These are people Australian governments seek to save from themselves; people it is safer to read about than live with.

If I am honest I am safer from those communities too. A clean home, food in the cupboard, safety and security, law and order are essential for health and happiness. But I know that world and I know what made that world and I know it is a world of hard choices and desperation. I know that world because I have seen it. This is the world that Australia prepared for me and I evaded it. But there I was in Mongolia wounded in any case and bound by fate to my community – my country.

PART SEVEN

I am above Australia now at 30,000 feet. Even from here I can feel the pull of this land: my land. I have woken from the steady hum of the plane as we pass over the red centre of Australia. It is always startling to me how the landscape resembles a dot painting. How remarkable it is that people who had never flown had such an intimate understanding of country. The art of central Australia expresses a sense of place from every angle. This is what 60,000 years has given us.

When I departed from Beijing – thousands of kilometres away – I had my headphones on. A song was playing, 'Walking in the Green Corn' by Grant-Lee Phillips – a native American singer – it talks about the simple joys of freedom and home. The lines of the song resonated deeply, though it wasn't corn I was returning to but canola and wheat. These are the colours and crops of my country. Soon I will be home.

Another song now plays in my head. It surprises me, it seems to have come from nowhere as I was staring at the dirt and spinifex far below. It is Archie Roach – an

Aboriginal singer and songwriter and to my mind one of the most beautifully pure voices this country has ever produced – singing the words of 'Beautiful Child'. I am lost in these lyrics of memory and tears.

Memory and tears: I was coming home to it all. Archie sang of the pain of our people. He was taken from his family as a boy and raised in foster homes. He had spent years lost and homeless. There were too many cold nights warmed with grog. He lived inside the darkness of our country. But Archie lit up this world and revealed the small lives that so many had never seen.

His song 'Took the Children Away' became the soundtrack of the Stolen Generations – 'snatched from their mother's breast said this was for the best – took them away'. Australians were opening their minds and hearts to people like Archie. How could anyone not? A gentle soul singing with no bitterness; this wasn't about politics, it was about people. Our humanity had been denied. Our children had been taken under a policy that believed they would be better off white. Archie brought them home. Soon a prime minister would apologise.

Listening to Archie always moved me to tears. It would come from deep within me. It was an open wound no space or distance could close. Archie's songs captured all of our experience: prison cells, missions, boxing tents, uncles and aunties, tarpaulin musters, Fitzroy and Redfern and

Musgrave Park. I knew this was real, because I knew these people; this, was me. I had gone so far from this world. I suppose I had wanted to escape it. But we never do.

At 30,000 feet flying over my country, I felt like that boy in Archie's song, growing up far too soon. I had grown up too soon, far beyond my young years. I was back now in Australia; back with those memories of the boy I used to be. There are moments that are locked away in some vault in my mind. I recall books I have read. I replay songs I have heard. Snatches of conversations from years ago can feel like yesterday. People long gone echo as if they are just in the next room.

Perhaps it is because I spent so much time alone as we moved from town to town that all of these disparate things resonate so deeply. I lived in my mind. Even among my siblings I felt a generation removed; thinking, staring out a car window at a world outside of our grasp. So we packed and unpacked. Sometimes I wished we would stop. My sister and I played a little game where we imagined a perfect life. We would ask what would we do when we finally got a home. She would talk about watching a colour television. I would dream about lounging on a new sofa. But this was just a fantasy. My reality was my family – a revolving door of cousins and aunties and uncles and that was ultimately enough.

Some towns stand out more than others. Some memories fill me with greater joy: riding my bike outside of Jindera or playing in the wheat silos or walking along the burning train tracks leading to the pool in Griffith. There are sad memories too: a friend who was electrocuted playing on the roof of his house or my neighbour who was accidentally shot and killed as he carried his rifle to hunt rabbits. But I never stayed long enough for any joy or sadness to linger. There was always another town. I just kept moving.

Eventually I found a place where I could breathe. It was far from my home. The world had unexpectedly opened up to me. For the first time in my life I felt free of race and history. Yes, these other countries had their own hatreds and divisions; many remained defined by what separated them: India and Pakistan, North and South Korea, Israel and Palestine. But there I was an observer. I didn't own these struggles. No longer did I meet people with wariness. I didn't have to suspect the motives of friends and colleagues. When asked where I was from I could answer Australia and be proud of it. When the inevitable follow up question came: what race are you? I could say I was an Aborigine and say it without caution. I had no concern about how these strangers would react because we didn't meet across the contested space of our shared past.

I have always been torn between the sadness of my history and the beauty of my country. Sometimes I can feel that the land itself understands this struggle. When I am alone by a river or driving across a plain I can hear this land talking to me, and it is always subdued. There is a magical connection that shows itself in unexpected ways. As I was writing this book, I received a handwritten letter. It was from a man who grew up on a property next to the Grant family homestead in Canowindra. This was the place built by my Irish convict ancestor on land he had seized from my black forebears. The man said he used to wander the land as a boy collecting old Wiradjuri artifacts. He said he had lost all of them except one. It was, he said, a beautiful stone axe and he wanted me to have it. I had never met this man. He had no idea I was writing this book. But I like to think that somehow my ancestors had chosen this moment through this man to talk to me. They wanted to be with me, to tell me that my connection to them could never be broken.

I have that axe now and it sits so comfortably in my hand. There is a groove where my thumb rests. It feels like it could have been made for me. I can imagine the painstaking hours spent smoothing its sides, grinding it to a fine point. It looks almost too good to use, more a piece of art than an implement. Perhaps it had been traded over time, passed from one hand to another until now it rests with me.

I called the man who sent it to me. He told me about growing up around Aboriginal kids. He went to school with them, played football alongside them. He said it wasn't until many years later he learned that the school bus didn't run to the missions; if the black kids wanted to go to school they had to walk in all weather. He said he realises now just how many obstacles were placed in their way, how many little things he took for granted that made life just that much more difficult for his Aboriginal schoolmates. He is saddened now, he says, to see the high levels of unemployment, the drinking and drugs that have ravaged that community. In that small way with that axe he had made his connection, given something back and for me opened a window into the generosity and spirit that can exist in our country.

Connections: these things that sustain me. I enjoy the little things, my family and music. I love to feel the sun in my face. I love the feel of diving into cool water. I love my mother's cooking. I love that my father is still with us. Nothing makes me more proud than to see my children with their friends – kids of all colours and backgrounds – comfortable and free. But I always find myself drawn back to the darkness. Sadness has always felt so much more familiar and so it is safer. We can live in its confines. We can laugh in its face. But it is preferable to happiness. Happiness feels like giving in, it feels like surrender. Happiness feels like the past is over and done and I am not yet ready for that.

* * *

Australia can be painful, but leaving for the first time, when I was in my early thirties, felt devastating. It seemed utterly unnatural. The night before my flight, I stood in the backyard of my cousin's house and stared at the sky. It was one of those warm autumn evenings before the cold begins to bite. Inside my family had gathered to say goodbye but I had always preferred the quiet moments alone with my thoughts. I could feel my heartbeat quickening with the realisation that in twenty-four hours I would be on the other side of the world. I wondered if it would look the same. Would the stars shine this bright? I knew there'd be no smell of eucalyptus and wattle. My cousin came up beside me. 'Will you miss it?' he asked. Yes. God, yes.

Nearly twenty years have passed since that night. I have seen war and death and disaster. I have met presidents and terrorists. I have seen inside countries cut off from the outside world. In these countries power controls people's minds. Armies grow strong while women and children starve. I have seen a country once considered the sick man of Asia re-emerge as a rival to the greatest superpower the world has ever known. Foreign affairs analysts are not wrong when they say the twenty-first century will be defined by the contest between China and America.

I had been liberated by the world. Out here I was a person, a man of strengths and weaknesses, with good days and bad but not a man pre-judged according to his race. I was working for one of the largest news networks on the planet. These were the greatest days of my career.

I worked with people from all over the world. My cameramen were Iranian and Canadian and British and Australian. My producers were Ethiopian and Chinese and Pakistani. These were my brothers and sisters and we would have laid down our lives for each other; I truly believe that.

I have known people who were killed in the field. One man who worked as an intermediary between the Taliban and us, who used to bring us videotapes, was murdered in his front driveway. Another reporter went missing to be found days later beaten to death and dumped on the road outside Islamabad. Reporters were kidnapped and tortured and beheaded. I made it back but I was not the person who left. I was battered and bent, probably broken in places. I had looked for an escape and found it in work and foreign places. Yet home – no matter how estranged I had felt – was always here. Now, 30,000 feet above my country, my head was filled with the songs of my people.

* * *

I had left Australia to pursue my career but also because I felt suffocated in this country. It must sound strange for you to hear me say that. I had enjoyed remarkable opportunities. I had moved far beyond the poverty of my youth. Equality was no longer an aspiration. To see me now compared to the young boy from the back roads of New South Wales, it would be easy to imagine that I had broken whatever chains bound me to my history. But as far as I had travelled I had carried my country – and its loss – with me.

When an anthem is played and a flag is raised we are reminded that this country is no longer ours – certainly not ours alone. I was overwhelmed by these feelings on the night Australia welcomed the world to the Olympic Games. It was a September evening, that time of the year when I think Sydney is at its best. The light has a golden hue and the people – sun seekers by nature – are shaking loose the last of winter's dark skies. The best of our country would be on show in the city where the modern nation of Australia began two centuries earlier. We built a stadium for this. Now the people came to fill it for the opening ceremony. I was there too – a face in the crowd – but feeling deeply alone.

This was a night of anthems and flags. I could pledge allegiance to neither. 'Australians all let us rejoice' had always rung hollow to me. What on earth did we have to rejoice? The theft of our land? The murder of our ancestors? The pillage and plunder of our culture and traditions? The destruction of our families? This anthem sounded more like a death march. The celebration, like dancing on our graves. My grandfather – my mother's father – a man who tried to find a way to live in the white world and who had loved a white woman, told me once that I didn't have to

183

stand up for this anthem. I had come home from school asking him why I had to recite the oath of loyalty to God, Queen and country. He said that wasn't for us. As I sat in that stadium, my loyalty was to his memory. I measured these people around me – with their pride in their flag and anthem – against their history and I knew that I wouldn't sing that song and I wouldn't cheer the Southern Cross.

My silent protest though did nothing to ease that ache inside me. There was a hole where my country should be. If I could I would sing in the loudest voice, my hand on my heart as the flag unfurled. I so want to believe. Love of country can inspire the hero inside us. It can call us to war. It can lead us onto the streets in protest when we believe our nation might fail us. Australians fight each other for what this country should be. They vote for the politics of their choice. They cheer for football teams that they inherit from their forebears. But as I looked around the Olympic stadium I realised that on this night they were one. They were an extended family: Australians all. This was their heritage and I didn't feel it belonged to me.

Where was my flag? Where was my anthem? All the nations of the world were here. One by one they marched into this cauldron. From Azerbaijan to Zimbabwe these people had forged their own destiny. They had their own histories and their scars to bear. They had shed blood. They had endured revolution. They were ruled by despots, kings and queens, and presidents. But they were their own people, marching under their own colours. I felt so empty. I am from a people with a heritage deeper than any on show before me that evening. We were the first seafarers. We found a home in an isolated continent cut off from the great land bridge to Africa. We are the oldest uninterrupted civilisation on earth. Yet, on this night we were nowhere. This was Australia's night under Australia's flag. The flag carried in its corner the Union Jack of Britain, an enduring symbol of our dispossession. The flag had excluded us, for so many years denying our citizenship. This was what colonisation meant and I had never felt it so deeply – I had never felt so powerless – as I did that night.

In the middle of this celebration of all that Australia proclaimed itself to be was a woman just like me. She came from a family that could trace its ancestry to the beginning of human time on this continent. Her family – like mine – had felt history's sting. Like me there were faces missing from her family album, people taken by the laws of a country that didn't want us here. Like me her face was a blend of other nations, but all of it fashioned into a fierce, defiant identity as a contemporary, aware indigenous person.

We were set apart from most of our black brothers and sisters. We were poster children for what Australia could do for our people. We were held up as examples of all that was possible. But this woman was also like me in another way – there was a part of her that this country could never claim. Cathy Freeman was about to light the flame that would ignite these games, to bind all the flags of the world under the banner of the Olympic Rings. She stood before this stadium to the cheers of a nation but her thoughts were with her people – they were always with her people. Cathy knew the history of this country – she had once said her people were slaves and prisoners trapped inside racist laws, they were fighters and so was she – and tattooed on her shoulder was her own personal deliverance – just three words: *'cos I'm free.*

Before the Olympic flame was doused Cathy would write her own history. In less than fifty seconds she fulfilled her destiny to claim gold in the 400 metres sprint. She was already world champion. She had dominated the event since her silver medal at the 1996 Atlanta games. This was the final mountain to climb with the weight of a nation's expectations and the history of her people.

There are moments when sport is greater than the field or track or stadium in which it is played. A horse named Phar Lap gave Australians hope in the Great Depression of the 1920s. Boxer Les Darcy – considered an inevitable world champion – united the nation in grief when he died so tragically young in America. Tens of thousands of people mourned his passing as his coffin made its journey from Sydney to his home in Newcastle. Another boxer Lionel

Rose – an Aborigine from Victoria – became the smiling face of the hope of the 1960s when he won the world title that had eluded Darcy. Then there are those whose feats are so great they personify who we are as a people. They are known as ours: 'our Dawn Fraser', 'our Don Bradman'. Now we had 'our Cathy'.

We watched her through different eyes as she took her place at the starting line. To Australians victory for this Aboriginal woman on this night would tell the world we had buried the old enmities. The stain of settlement could be wiped clean. We – my people, Cathy's people – saw her as a symbol of survival. She told the world we were still here. For the woman herself this was a race like so many others – a track, a starter's gun and a finish line – but then it was unlike any other. When she crossed that line there was just the earth and she sank into it. She stared into space – seemingly oblivious to the crowd – unburdened. Then she rose to her feet and here was the moment when the flag of our people was unfurled. Red, black and yellow flew in this stadium and its image was beamed around the world. I thought back to the opening ceremony and how I felt alone and now how proud I was and I cried.

I felt transformed that night in the Olympic stadium. Our people had been on the losing end of history but Cathy made us all feel like winners. I allowed myself that moment – we all did. But this was a myth and myths can crumble at the touch. The myth of Cathy Freeman could never truly sustain us. She was a runner who became a champion but *'cos I'm free* does not mean her people are. Gold – even this most precious and dazzling gold – ultimately dims. Cathy's glory is frozen in time but as the memories fade of that stunning night our people are still a nation without an anthem or a flag that can fly at the Olympic Games.

* * *

I had struggled with the history of my own country for so long and living overseas gave me a chance to loosen that yoke from my neck. No matter where I went though I found myself looking for some validation of who I was. Identity is a two-way street – we need others to see us as we see ourselves. I found myself gravitating to locals in Pakistan and Afghanistan. There was kinship there, an innate understanding. These were tribal people and they saw the world as I did. They had a deep connection to their land. My cameraman was Iranian and his family had been shaped by the turbulent and violent history of his country and we bonded profoundly. We enjoyed breaking away from the western media pack and eating street food with local people.

I clung to who I was: I was still an Aboriginal man. But over time I drifted further from my country and my people. I never forgot who I was. But out here in the world it just didn't matter as much. The demands of work – the adventures of life – were all consuming. Soon thoughts didn't turn as readily to home. People I loved receded to a deeper corner of my mind – always a warm comforting place to visit but I just didn't live there anymore.

Relationships – even those dearest to me – began to fade. I suppose I always felt that home was there waiting for my return. But time does not stand still: people live and die. I would receive news from home about a cousin or uncle who had passed away. I would grieve not just for their loss, but for the loss I felt in those moments for my country. But I was so far away and life moved so quickly. I didn't go home for my grandmother's funeral. My mother's mother – that blonde-haired, blue-eyed woman who had dared to cross Australia's colour line – had meant the world to me. Now I was in Beijing or Islamabad or Pyongyang – I can't even recall where – and my nan was being laid to rest. I feel condemned by that and I have to live with it. Nothing could illustrate more just how distant I had become.

Is this what can happen? Can an indigenous person formed in his land find another home far, far away? I was always certain my identity was bound in land and family and history. None of that was true here, so who was I? Perhaps I could stay away forever, Australia relegated to a place of memory.

I am often asked: What is an identity? It is a question that defies one convenient answer. Identity is forever in flux. Yet, there are those things that are essential to us: the permanence of family and the traditions of culture. Our history shapes us, and for my people there is the legacy of racism. But indigenous identity has been especially fraught, something inherently political. I shouldn't have to explain myself at all, but in Australia we have never had that privilege. It should be enough to say I am a man of a Wiradjuri father and a Kamilaroi mother, a man who draws his ancestry too from white Australia. But my identity comes from navigating the space in between and having to explain that to an often uncomprehending, sceptical – even hostile – nation.

In this space we brush against each other. We touch and talk and love. But still there is a space. We fill this space with language. We talk about us and them or black and white. We fill this space with hate and charity. We fill the space with ignorance and fear. It is the space on a bus: an empty seat, a black face and a hesitation: should I sit there?

It is a space in a classroom or on a sporting field. The space we feel compelled to fill with having to be twice as good. It is the space filled with a blue light and a uniform.

It is in the choking fear that can so easily rise in my people when we see that blue light. It is a reflex action, just for a moment: did I do something wrong?

This space between us we don't talk about. We measure it in numbers: the lowest life expectancy, the highest infant mortality, the highest imprisonment rate, the highest unemployment, the worst health, housing and education. These are the numbers of faces we never see. Here is another number: six out of ten Australians have never met their black countrymen, many wouldn't even know if they had.

Why choose to say I am this and not the other? Some imagine it as a supposed struggle between our white and black ancestry, as if choosing one repudiates the other. This logic always seems to assume our 'whiteness' should triumph. The identity of so-called 'mixed-race' people is especially challenged; our facial features or colouring divined as if there is some diminishing scale of Aboriginality. I understand how to people not familiar with us we can be confounding. The image of an Aborigine is fixed in the popular imagination; shaped by too many Eric Jolliffe cartoons of 'Witchetty's Tribe' or spear-carrying black garden gnomes on white suburban lawns.

In Australia our identity has always been contested. It is there in the sixty-seven different government definitions that I wrote about earlier. It is there in comments such as: 'You're too pretty to be Aboriginal' or 'You're too smart to be Aboriginal' – yes, ask any indigenous person, we have all heard these back-handed offensive 'compliments'. This is the hangover of the old colonial perceptions of us as brutish sub-humans.

We are often told we should all just be Australians. It is a noble sentiment, and perhaps one day we can find a common identity that encompasses us all, but for much of this country's history we have been told we were anything but Australian. We have been told what an Australian is and we know so often, in so many ways, we are not that. We die ten years younger than other Australians. We are twelve times more likely to be locked up. Over the age of forty, we are six times more likely to go blind. Indigenous children are said to have the highest rates of deafness in the world. Indigenous people are three times more likely to be jobless than other Australians.

Australia has universal health care, a minimum living wage and if unemployment tips over six per cent it warrants front-page headlines. If Australia is free, prosperous and healthy then we are not Australians. This doesn't happen by accident, there is nothing racially programmed in us that would mean we are predestined to fail. This is what Australia has created.

Racism ties us in knots. White Australia has made us black by telling us we are not white. Yet for much of our history Australian policy was based around assimilation –

absorbing us into white society. To be black – to be part of indigenous culture – is not simply about skin colour. My family ranges from chocolate to alabaster. But we are a people; we share a bloodline and a history.

When I was a boy my world was alive with stories. We told ourselves who we were by keeping alive the memories of those passed. In my family's telling, time was not important – what happened yesterday was as real today and would be again tomorrow. What happened to my forebears felt as real as if it had happened to me. The pain of dispossession and suffering became printed on my DNA. Doctors talk about epigenetic inheritance: the experiences of parents and grandparents passed directly to their offspring. Some families carry genetic illness, passed down through the generations. My people inherit the loss of our country. It has proven as incurable and potentially lethal as any cancer.

* * *

Some argue that there should be no racial divisions among people. I agree, but again we weren't responsible for dividing us in the first place. The black American writer Ta-Nehisi Coates says racism is the father of race, not the other way around. It is true; there is no such thing as race. There is no science that divides humans according to hair and skin.

It is notions of racial superiority that have separated us; placed one above another.

We are all variations on those same modern humans who first walked out of Africa. Our journeys took us to different parts of the world. We know now that geography, climate and diet helped shape physical appearance and skin colour. By studying the fossilised remains of ancient Europeans and mapping the genome of modern people, geneticists have recently been able to peer back thousands of years to see societies and peoples in transformation. Ten thousand years ago most of the people of Europe were dark skinned. But these scientists claim that as agriculture spread and people began living more sedentary lives they changed, their very molecular structure was altered. New variants of genes evolved to aid the digestion of new foods and milk. Over time the changes resulted in lightening skin, and these farming people mixed with others, leading to Europeans today.

Jared Diamond's seminal book *Guns, Germs, and Steel* argued persuasively that people are born with similar and equal capacities but access to fertile land and deep river systems led to agriculture and trade, eventually improving technology, and the development of better weapons. With the arrival of British ships on this land, guns, germs and steel would wreak havoc on my ancestors.

The point of this is that we are not separate species; we are all *Homo sapiens*. But the appearance of 'racial' differences has always proved irresistible. Ancient Egyptians, Greeks, Romans and Chinese claimed superiority over people with lighter or darker skin. The age of exploration gave rise for further divisions. By the seventeenth and eighteenth centuries scientists began to speak of several 'races' of humans, as if they were entirely separate species. Skulls would be examined to determine supposed levels of intelligence.

There is nothing genetic that separates us; what divides us is our history – what we have done to each other in the name of race. It is this racism that persists so powerfully in our imaginations. Racism benchmarks civilisation and ranks us all in order. Racism justified taking everything from us.

* * *

Over time exclusion hardens into political opposition. As I grew older I grew stronger in my resolve. I would not be told who I was. I looked to my father and his father before him. They were the people who defined me and they were not white nor did they wish to be. I looked to my white grandmother and what she endured to love an Aboriginal man and raise Aboriginal kids.

I looked to the new Aboriginal political movement that demanded land rights and equal wages and full citizenship. I looked to our flag – black for the people, red for the earth and the blood spilled upon it and the yellow sun – to bind us as one. I wore that flag and marched behind it as we took our voice to the street.

Still, as much as I sought to fortify my sense of self, we can't help but be fragile. Our identities are often not sheets of armour but an eggshell that can shatter at your touch. There have been times when I have believed what Australians have said about me. I have been ashamed of who I am. And I am ashamed to admit that because I come from strong people.

I come from men with broad backs and women with big hearts. I come from men who fought wars for this country and women who scrubbed the floors of white people to feed their families. I come from people locked out of education but who taught themselves to read and passed their love of words to me.

All of this is the journey of identity forged out of the settlement of Australia. An identity carved up, measured and fought over. I grapple too with inconsistencies and contradictions. Even before I left Australia I had begun to wrestle with my place among my people. It wasn't a question of whether I belonged, but how to express that sense of belonging. Too often I would see our identity couched in terms of suffering and poverty and that felt incomplete. The reality of my life was in the starkest contrast to where I had started and where so many indigenous people remained.

How do we define identity when it can become so fractured? In an earlier book *The Tears of Strangers* I wrote of how confounding it can be to live as an indigenous person in a society – black society – now lacerated by class, gender and geography.

I wrote of how the old definitions of Aboriginality strain to serve the constellation of groups and individuals that lay claim to that identity. It is something other marginalised, impoverished minority groups wrestle with as they try to transcend the gaze of race to look to other factors. Those inconsistencies were sharpened the longer I remained away from Australia.

I still find myself uneasily charting a course between personal success and the plight of my people. I have escaped the poverty of my childhood yet so many remain trapped in misery. I see this on the streets where I live. A regular, quiet night having dinner or catching a movie can be punctured by the sight of my family – my cousins, my own blood – begging for food or money. I am confronted with the contradiction of the promise of Australia – a promise I have seized – and the reality of my people. It can make my good fortune feel unseemly.

Here is my choice: my fork in the road. Do I turn my head and hurry past, hoping we don't catch each other's eyes? To be honest, I sometimes feel like that. It is easier than being confronted with such misery. I could avoid that awkward conversation, that meeting of family and kinship that can feel like a pretence; that will end with me walking away, and them cajoling the next passerby. But I stop – cuz, brother, sister – we share the familiar greetings, we hug and in a few minutes I will slip them some cash and go on my way.

In me – people like me – who have carved out a space for ourselves in Australia, we can imagine a future for all indigenous people. This is a more comforting, hopeful story, the story of a steady march of progress. But it is so easily shattered. The facts of black lives just don't support it. That I am on television, earn a good living and send my kids to good schools, does not redeem our history. It is as illogical as saying Julia Gillard becoming Australia's first female Prime Minister vanquished sexism. Of course it is a step forward, but the fact that it is exceptional reminds us how far we have to go, how far apart we are in this country.

As I touched down now – once again home where I truly belonged – I felt reconnected to this country. Soon though, I would be reminded that this country I had been raised in, this country I had loved and left – Australia – could still bring my people to their knees.

PART EIGHT

I am standing at ground zero. This is a place at the foot of the spiritual centre of our country. Here, in 2007, in the shadow of the rock – Uluru – the army moved in, telling the local people they were here to save them. Mutitjulu was the first target of the so-called intervention. The then Howard government responded to what it saw as a crisis. The media was awash with stories of violence and abuse. There were reports of young children being targeted by gangs of paedophiles. Communities were under siege, reeling from alcohol and drug use. Pornography was said to be rampant. A report was released, 'Little Children are Sacred', commissioned by the Northern Territory Government. It highlighted what it saw as a lack of government action. The authors described the situation as one of 'urgent national significance'.

The Federal Government called in the troops. Army and police seized control of seventy-three Northern Territory remote communities. It was a taskforce of more than 600 cops and soldiers. Removed now from the urgency of the times and the screaming headlines, it seems so absurd, so insensitive that the government thought to roll in such a heavy show of force on a people who for generations had lived under the often brutal hand of such authority. But these were different and, we were told, desperate times.

The *Racial Discrimination Act* was set aside. The Australian Constitution gives the Federal Government the power to make laws based on race. Now the homes of Aboriginal people could be entered at will. Alcohol bans were imposed, welfare payments were quarantined and managers were appointed to run communities. The people were powerless to stop it. Some Aboriginal voices were raised in protest. To them this intervention was a land grab, dispossession all over again with the lives of little children used as cover. But the indigenous community itself was divided. Strong voices argued this action was long overdue. They supported the intervention. Communities, they said, were at risk, women and children were being brutalised; it was time for something drastic.

I watched this story unfold from afar, reporting to the world from my home in the Middle East. I too was horrified by the stories of rape and bashings. I was not blind to the dysfunction in some communities. I had reported on it. In the 1990s I had travelled to a community in western New South Wales that was in the grip of a deadly spiral. There had been suicides. Grog and drugs were tearing lives apart. A lawyer representing an indigenous client said if things did not change, the entire community would be wiped out in a generation. I found children as young as ten drinking openly from flagon bottles. There were wild brawls outside the local pub. In the 1970s this community was chosen for a new housing project; now those same houses were condemned. Up to twenty people were crammed into small living spaces.

It was a recipe for collapse and it was all so depressingly familiar. To outside eyes this was a failure of the people themselves. But we know that this is the legacy of history and generations of poor government policies. Money is spent, houses are built, new programs are devised and the malaise deepens. With each new era of policy – protection, integration, assimilation or self-determination – the problem remains the same; communities themselves are rendered powerless with limited input into how they run their lives. When indigenous bodies have been formed they have been prone to collapse under mismanagement or the weight of bureaucracy. It is a sad fact too that unscrupulous, predatory individuals exploit and rip off their own people. In this, we are no different from governments, unions or corporations anywhere.

Now, the intervention was being imposed top down. Communities were not consulted. This was not how it was meant to be: the report that helped spark this crackdown had specifically recommended that communities be involved. Years later the indigenous expert who co-wrote the 'Little Children are Sacred' report, Pat Anderson, lashed out at the intervention describing it as 'neither well intentioned nor well evidenced'. She said it was based on ignorance and prejudice and disempowered people, which only worsened their problems. She accused the government of devising the whole operation on the back of an envelope.

As I stood in Mutitjulu I was at the crossroads of the eternal dilemma in indigenous affairs. How do we redress generations of disadvantage and injustice? How do we protect people from violence and abuse? How do we build secure, healthy communities? Most critically, how can this be done when the people themselves – those who abuse and suffer abuse – have been so beaten down? I am not a politician. I am a storyteller. I try to connect people to our shared humanity. When I looked around Mutitjulu – my first weekend back in my country after years away – I realised that I had seen better, more functional refugee camps in war zones than this.

I was angry and I was sad. I looked around and saw people sitting aimlessly outside their dilapidated homes. Alcohol was supposedly banned but broken bottles and empty cans were littered inside upturned cars. I peered inside one to see bottles of bourbon and when I looked closer the decaying carcass of a dead dog. The skin was lifted from the skeleton and its snout was exposed, baring its teeth in what looked like a menacing grin. If any image summed up this collision of community, neglect and government policy this was it. The dog was having the last twisted laugh.

I had come out to the centre of Australia to launch National Indigenous Television. The fledgling network was going national, linking with SBS to bring our stories to an Australian audience. In this way Australia had changed for the good. More indigenous kids were completing high school; more were graduating from university. The numbers of doctors, lawyers, architects and engineers were on the rise. When I had left Australia I was one of the very few indigenous journalists. We were largely absent from the nation's TV screens. We didn't feature in advertising campaigns or star in major movie releases. Now, performers like Gurrumul could fill the Sydney Opera House; movies like *The Sapphires* – about an indigenous singing group that toured war-torn Vietnam – could set box office records and win awards. Actors like Deborah Mailman and Aaron Pedersen were household names. We were winning *Australian Idol*. Now there was a new generation of storytellers with our own television network.

Politicians and rock stars turned up for the big day. I had spent the morning with my old friend, actor Ernie

Dingo. Ernie and I had met around my mother's kitchen table thirty years earlier. I was still in school and Ernie was setting out on his career. He was a friend of my sister and even then I knew this was a unique character, quick witted and charismatic. We talk about that day whenever we meet, how two young Aboriginal men lived their dreams. Troy Cassar-Daley, the award-winning country musician, was performing, and seeing him again I was reminded of his easy smile and his pure joy being around his own people. Troy has always reminded me of the boys I grew up with, just straight-up down-to-earth blackfellas. I was co-hosting the launch with another dear friend Rhoda Roberts. Rhoda had blazed a trail in the media, presenting news and current affairs programs on SBS. All of us – Ernie, Troy, Rhoda and me – were united in kinship. We came from different parts of the country – different nations, different families – but as indigenous people we transcended all of that. We could look at each other and with a nod or a smile bind ourselves to history, pain, and survival.

That night I stood under a blanket of stars in the heart of my country. After years away I wanted to pull down the sky and wrap it around me. I found myself throughout that day kicking at the dirt to raise the dust and have it spill over my boots and settle on the cuffs of my jeans. I wanted to carry this country physically on my body. I had sat in the sun and felt it draw my spirit out from deep inside me, reconnecting to my place. No foreign sun had warmed me like this. In the background Frank Yamma sang, 'Find me another way to die.' His powerful voice echoed across this place and spanned the distance between the celebration I was a part of and the numbing reality of life on the other side of the rock. We had every right to be proud of NITV, to find pleasure in being together, but it sat so uneasily with the dead dogs and empty bottles I had seen just that morning in Mutitjulu. And here was the contradiction of our country, it invites us in – it celebrates our success – and it condemns us still to misery.

And Frank Yamma's song trailed off into the darkness: 'Find me another way to live.'

* * *

'What does it feel like to be an indigenous person in Australia?'

I am standing in a radio studio in Sydney trying to explain why it is that we are so vulnerable and exposed in our own country. The interviewer – ABC's Richard Glover – I have always found a gentle soul. His interviews are less about what divides us; at his best he looks to knit together the frayed fibres of our shared humanity. He has learned first hand that what we do to each other can come from something missing or damaged in ourselves. He has also learned one of the most valuable lessons of life, that we are better than our worst. He has written eloquently of his own journey into his troubled family and how it has shaped him. It lends Richard empathy and there is softness in his question that is comforting and disarming.

What does it feel like?

I could resort to moral outrage. I could recite the litany of injustice and brutality that has been visited on my people. I could roll out that endless list of damning statistics that always ends in that same mantra: we are the most impoverished, disadvantaged people in the country. All of this would be true. I could speak with anger throwing up words like guilt and shame and blame. In this too I would not be wrong. But I find myself searching for something else.

I have grown beyond the angry student of my youth. I have had to confront my own failings so it is not hard to understand, even forgive the failings of others. Australia is bigger than us all and we only hold it for a brief moment before handing it to our children. I suppose I am a diplomat by nature; I seek equilibrium and balance. In this I am the essence of my astrological sign, Libra. More than that there is harsh pragmatism; we are only a fraction of this country's population and if we can't speak to the country as a whole then I fear we are doomed. As I look for the words to try to answer Richard's question, I seek the language of healing because we just can't take any more pain.

I tell Richard how vulnerable we can be. I tell him of the little boy I once was who felt so ashamed of his colour that he tried to scrub it off. I tell him of the ache of poverty and how my family had roamed the back roads looking for a home in a land we had lost. I tell him of how a sideways glance or a snickering child could steal our souls. I tell him how we have learned to measure our words and lower our voices for fear of being howled down. I tell him that even now despite carving out a place for myself I could so easily be crushed by rejection. And he listens. He gives me the space to find these words and he lets them settle.

As I speak my mind reaches back through the years. At times I swallow hard and feel my heart beat that fraction quicker. I find a space at the back of the studio and fix my gaze, occasionally glancing away when my voice catches and a tear forms. At these moments I am with my mother and father; I am seated on the steps on a sunny day with my grandfather circling the tips on his racing form guide. I am flicking towels and dunking my friends – black brothers all – on an egg-frying hot day at the Griffith swimming pool. I feel them all with me and know that I am never alone and what I say speaks for them too.

My life had led me to this point. A boy who grew up with a love of words, who sat at the feet of his parents and heard stories of struggle and survival, was now being asked to speak to his country. I felt this responsibility heavily and I had come to it reluctantly. But old wounds were being reopened. I had grown up with the legacy of Australian racism and here it was rearing its head again. We – Australians black and white – meet each other across the gulf of our history. If I was being called to this story then it came from my ancestors: it came from my great grandfather Bill Grant – a man born of black and white, a man whose name I read on the roll call of people from Bulgandramine mission. I was following the tradition of a man they called the storyteller.

* * *

In the winter of 2015 Australia turned to face itself. The comforting myths and convenient lies no longer seemed to hold. We were perplexed and confused. Some were angry. Others were defiant. Old wounds were being torn open. These were the wounds of my countrymen. These were the wounds we hoped no one could see.

This was the winter when headlines blazed and voices roared with fury. We were being tested; all of that which Australia had constructed: that ANZAC spirit; Kokoda; bushfire, flood and drought toughness. All that we held as uniquely ours, mateship and tolerance. We had never believed that, my people. We knew a different sunburnt country. We knew disease and death, poverty and police lock-ups. We knew fringe town camps and grog on the riverbank, and bloodied boxing tents.

In the winter of 2015, these two versions of Australia collided. It happened in that place where we are told we are all truly equal; that place most hallowed and sacred to us. It happened on the sporting field. The football is meant to be a place where we can disappear; we blend into one another. A siren sounds, lines are drawn and the colours of our teams unite us. Here we find our heroes and people rich and poor, men and women, young and old have a voice the same as the person beside them.

From the hill to the stands to the corporate box we yield our own small existence to morph into something much bigger: a team. We are born into our teams, colours bequeathed down through the generations, bound by past glory and fortified by defeat. Our teams bring us together; whatever may separate us, for that moment we are one. We stand as a team against other teams, and we cheer – thousands of voices together.

But in the winter of 2015 we didn't cheer. There was another sound; a sound that had been building for years; that had started on one voice in a crowd until it seemed to become the crowd itself. With each passing week it spread from ground to ground as it grew louder, a contagion obscuring meaning or motive. Some still clung to the idea that this was sport; our collective pressure valve, and it would subside on the final siren. But, it didn't. It grew in venom, touching something primal.

That sound came from our history. An Australia that was born on a fleet and a flag and had come to riches on wool, and the earth had not reckoned with its darker legacy, not really. It touched our guilt or our shame or our ignorance or our plain bigotry. If our national passion for sport had given us a common identity then now, that was being laid bare.

At the centre of it all was a man who was told he was Australian. This man was hailed a hero. He was not just any Australian; he was Australian of the Year. He believed he was Australian – he described himself as an assimilated man. But Australia has always been an uncomfortable fit for us. Indigenous people sit uneasily in the national imagination. We were the people with chains around our necks – we were Truganini, the Tasmanian we were told was the last of her doomed race, and Albert Namatjira who painted the heart of our nation and was given full citizenship and voting rights before his countrymen and women and was then jailed for allegedly supplying alcohol to his people and died soon after. Now, we were Adam Goodes.

* * *

Somewhere inside us all is the child who never grows; that truest part of ourselves, free to dream before adulthood shapes us, bends us to the will and ignorance and expectations of others. For me – that place will always be a small town in western New South Wales; a town with a main street and a Greek café and a bakery. It will always be a riverbank and the smell of eucalyptus after rain. It will always be the backseat of a car with my family huddled inside carrying all that we own.

Away back in time in another small New South Wales town, there was a boy who would grow into a champion. Here a skinny, loose-limbed, brown-skinned boy dreamed of playing soccer for his country. The round ball was never out of his hand. It had been his one constant as he trudged from town to town, the uncertainty of life hanging heavily over his fractured family.

He had moved with his mother and younger brothers, fleeing a marriage in tatters, and the ghosts of the past buried deep in the troubled racial history of this country. There was never a home – never one place that he could be still. But the ball he carried was his escape. When all else failed him that ball could take him away from it all.

Adam Goodes never did become a soccer player. He grew tall and strong and the ball changed shape but his dream never dimmed. He would become one of the greatest Australian Rules footballers of his generation –

an indigenous man playing an indigenous game, a game that was born here. Adam's greatness is measured in the way that sport gauges greatness, in numbers. He was twice awarded the Brownlow Medal – recognition as the game's player of the year. Four times he has been named an all-Australian representative. He has two AFL premierships. He has been selected in the Australian indigenous team of the century.

But these numbers tell only a part of Adam's story. There is another number that haunts us all and speaks to something much deeper than sporting glory: 50,000, the number of children taken – stolen – from their families. Adam's mother was one of them.

Adam Goodes is sitting across from me, a man at the apex of success, looking back along a road long travelled. We have come together for an interview for the National Indigenous Television program *Awaken*. We are two indigenous men who have wrestled with the contradictions of our country and Australia's legacy of racism. We bond over a pain shared; an estrangement from our nation; separated by skin and history from our fellow Australians. If we are honest we have to admit, we sometimes sit uneasily too among our own people.

Nearly twenty years separates Adam and me, but we have trodden similar paths. I hear him when he tells me of his search for identity. I see him like me – in all those small towns – always moving with his mother and brothers, looking for that place to belong.

'Mum left Dad when I was about ten. We moved from Adelaide to Wallaroo and sort of kept moving around. We went to about five or six different primary schools growing up; three different high schools. We were never sort of stuck in any one spot,' he tells me.

Adam's mother Lisa had been searching all her life, looking for an identity that had been taken from her. Adam told me of his mother's broken past. She was part of that generation lost. She was another black child offered up to the great Australian idea, that with just enough white in them they could be civilised and saved from the predicted doom of their forebears.

We know of the tragic outcome of that misguided – some say well-intentioned – policy. These were lives crushed by an unbearable whiteness. Children: in homes – sometimes even loving homes – often destined never to truly know themselves. The government inquiry into the Stolen Generations – the 'Bringing Them Home' report – makes for heartbreaking reading. We have known this in my family. Adam's mother lived it.

In 2008 then Prime Minister Kevin Rudd apologised for our nation's treatment of these children. He has told me how he wrote the speech himself in long hand. He wanted to feel close to these words – from his pen to the nation's heart. Rudd is seen now as a divisive figure, a plotter and schemer who contributed to one of the most volatile and treacherous eras in our political history. But this moment – the apology – was above politics. He spoke to indigenous people who had borne the pain of separation and found the words for what he called 'this blemished chapter in our nation's history'. The apology helped ease pain: just the fact of acknowledgement; just to say this happened and we are sorry dressed an open wound. But the lives of people like Lisa were by then irrevocably shaped and too often damaged. These were people who would never get home again.

Lisa searched and took her boys with her. There was one broken marriage, followed by another; and there was violence. Adam told me of the nights of restless sleep, hoping the arguments would stop, of his little brothers' fears.

'Hearing them fight all the time, it was quite annoying and I know my younger brothers were scared by it. I saw it as a way to stop them fighting by sneaking out and calling the police,' he said.

Adam has searched for his own answers. He campaigns against family violence. He champions reconciliation. This is his personal quest; a quest to understand his mother and her pain and answer the question that has always gnawed at him: who am I?

'Growing up, I knew I was different. I knew I was Aboriginal. I just didn't know what it meant to be Aboriginal,' Adam said.

I have said throughout this book how we all look for stories that make sense of our world. As a boy I felt our poverty, our restlessness; I measured our lives on the fringes against the lives of my white schoolmates and wondered: what put us here? I had a family strong in its sense of itself and parents who filled my imagination with the funny and sad stories of just being black.

Adam looked to his mother for answers, and found more questions.

'There was obviously no culture, no language, no cultural practices. Even just connection to my other Aboriginal family members was really hard,' he told me.

Adam's father was white and even though he was no longer around, it marked him as different among other blacks. We can be cruel. Communities under stress often turn on each other. I had seen that growing up. I had seen how we could hurt each other – brutally at times – because there was no one else left to hurt. Adam felt this. Other Aborigines called him 'coconut' – brown on the outside but white on the inside.

His mother told him to ignore the taunts, stay in school and get an education. 'You're bettering yourself,' she said, 'in ten years' time you will come back here and they will still be doing the same thing.'

Lisa carried a much deeper fear. A woman who had been removed from her family knew the welfare officers stalked her children too. She would not let them take her boys.

'She made all these sacrifices and made sure we went to school and had lunch packed and breakfast before we left. There was no doubt she was thinking that she didn't want the government to come and take her kids away, and that was the one thing she was going to give us boys, a better opportunity,' he said.

Adam spoke of a love for Lisa that mirrors mine for my mother. As my mother sacrificed for me, Adam's took every step with him to school, took every kick on the footy field and when the time came, packed his bags, drove him to the airport and told him to come home with a premiership.

Here was the dream of a boy with a ball. On the field everything fell away, all those questions receded at least for that moment; that moment when instinct triumphed over intellect. Adam knew that he played his best football when he was in the moment.

The Sydney Swans saw that talent. They saw his potential as an athlete, but they also saw the man he could become. But there were hard lessons to learn. Adam admits he was lazy, not mentally tough enough or prepared to sacrifice in order to succeed. It came to a head after what he thought was a successful season. Adam was left out of the Swan's leadership group. His own teammates had voted and they didn't include him.

Adam told me how that cut him, but it made him grow up. He spoke to the coach, who told him what he needed to do. He was told to lift his consistency, to challenge other players and himself. The coach also told him to find his voice; he wanted to hear Adam. A man who had learned as a boy to keep his head down, now needed to stand tall and loud. The next year he was voted the best player in the AFL: a prestigious Brownlow Medal. He made the leadership group and has remained there ever since.

If Adam found his self on the field, away from football he searched for his identity. The questions that followed him through childhood remained. Adam began a Diploma of Aboriginal Studies, deepening his knowledge of history and politics. Again, it is a path I know too well. I came to university in Sydney at an age similar to when Adam joined the Swans. Like me, Adam grew angry as he learned the truth of this country and how it had treated our people.

'That really was a sad, sad journey, learning about Aboriginal history and massacres, and youth suicide and health problems and employment problems. There was a time I was really angry at people who were not Aboriginal and I really had problems dealing with it,' he said.

Still, there was football.

Anger can be energy and Adam now used it to motivate himself. Where his mother had limited opportunities, Adam would touch the sky, in his case literally. His speed and anticipation and his ability to soar above the heads of other players thrilled football fans. He delivered that promised premiership to his mother and added another. He won a second Brownlow Medal.

Adam Goodes had every reason to believe he was free of the shackles of the past. He still grappled with Australia's history and the treatment of his people, but at least he had found acceptance. In Adam the policy of assimilation was made real. This is how he saw himself; he described himself as an assimilated man.

'I am mainstream Australia,' he said, 'whether I am indigenous or not.'

This is the sadness of Adam Goodes. This is how the rejection hurt. Australia asks us to believe – we are told to put our history behind us. We are told that with success will come peace and acceptance. I knew this because I had been tempted too. I had sought to put distance between blackness and me; to find a place where history could not touch me. I had gone as far from this country and the back roads of my childhood as I could. But we don't escape ourselves and when your roots run so deep in this land it will call you home.

I returned to an Australia that was still fighting old battles. Still bound in old attitudes. Still harbouring a deep, festering racism. For all the good will, the apologies and reconciliation, the wounds of our history could tear open at any moment.

On 24 May 2013 Adam Goodes, assimilated Aboriginal man, came face to face with a bigotry rooted in the Australian imagination. It came from a thirteen-year-old girl but it echoed from a darker time, in attitudes formed about Aborigines at first glance; the belief that we were primitive and savage, barely human.

Now on a football field in Melbourne, Adam Goodes was reminded how we have not thrown off those ugly attitudes – how it is imprinted deep in our psyche: Adam was called an ape by a thirteen-year-old girl in the crowd. This was another chapter in a game with a sordid racial history. A former Collingwood AFL club president Allan McAlister once said Aborigines were welcome at his club as long as they conducted themselves like white people.

There is a contradiction in football; it has opened its doors to black footballers. They make up nearly ten per cent of AFL playing rosters. But attitudes like McAlister's were embedded in the game's culture. This is the game that drove St Kilda indigenous star Nicky Winmar to lift his shirt and point to his skin in defiance of racial taunts in 1993.

Two years later Essendon player Michael Long protested at racial taunts from rival Damian Monkhorst. His stand forced the AFL to change its rules, introducing an anti-vilification policy. He and Monkhorst forged a new friendship and campaigned to change attitudes.

Adam Goodes may have thought those battles had been fought and won. He was wrong.

He took a stand and was praised. In 2014 he was named Australian of the Year. Now, here was a platform to use the voice his coach had told him to find. He spoke of our shared past. He worked for reconciliation, but one that was built on recognition of the suffering of people like his mother.

Adam Goodes was no longer just jumper number 37, Sydney Swans footballer. This was a new, strident, provocative man who mixed politics and sport – that oil and water of Australian society – and the mood soured.

Then in the winter of 2015 it started. A jeer in a corner of a stadium grew to a crescendo of boos. Week after week, Adam Goodes faced this maddening chorus.

What drove it? Some said they simply did not like him. To others he was a cheat, staging for free kicks. But there was something more sinister here. There was a line between Adam Goodes and the thirteen-year-old girl and the ape taunt and this vocal lynching. Adam Goodes had moved beyond his station; he was a blackfella with a voice talking to a country that didn't like what it heard.

Now, the man who had scaled the heights of his game who had won every accolade it had to offer retreated – broken.

Australians could no longer look away from this mirror, from what this showed to us. This was no longer a story of politics. This was a story we read in the grandstands and we could no longer ignore it.

Some in the media tried to paint Adam as the villain. They twisted his words and accused him of humiliating the thirteen year old who vilified him. He did no such thing.

Australians manned their barricades: some genuinely perplexed and saddened; others outraged that this country could even be accused of racism. He was accused of playing the victim; dealing the race card.

Adam was told to toughen up. Get over it. We hear this a lot. History is in the past, bad things happened but it is time to move on.

But history is not past for us.

Adam returned to the field and the booing subsided, but it never truly silenced. Now Adam Goodes – number 37 – has left the arena for the final time. Somewhere there is a child in all of us. Adam Goodes is still the boy with a ball. Still a boy who stepped up. Still a boy who dreamed. For all of his greatness and all of his achievement, Adam Goodes is still a boy who asks: who am I?

In the winter of 2015, we asked: who are we?

I am at the northern tip of our country, looking out at the coastline where my ancestors' journey to this land began 60,000 years ago. This is the land of the Yolngu of Arnhem Land. These are strong people; language and culture and story is alive here. At these times I ponder our separate fates. My people – the Wiradjuri – felt the full impact of British invasion: disease and the gun. We adapted and formed a new society out of this collision. Here the Yolngu were far from the site of first settlement; the arc of white Australia took longer to reach them. They have felt its sting – no doubt – but it has been more gradual than the cataclysmic clash of the southern states.

We talk of a pan-Aboriginal identity and it is true, but we are also very different. I am aware that here I am a guest, a man in a foreign land but I am not a stranger. I am among my people and I need to be. This is the Garma Festival, an annual event organised by the Yolngu that brings leaders of political and corporate Australia together with indigenous people. We come from all over Australia to share in a celebration of survival and to try to find new paths forward.

The shadow of the Adam Goodes saga hangs heavily over the meetings this year. Little children have drawn the number 37 on their arms in solidarity with their football hero. Every discussion begins with an acknowledgment of the pain this is causing our people. The day before I had bumped into Mick Gooda, the Human Rights Commission Aboriginal and Torres Strait Islander Social Justice Commissioner. The sun had still not risen and we were looking for an early morning coffee at Darwin airport awaiting our flight to Gove Peninsula. Mick is normally a garrulous irrepressible man, that day he was more solemn: 'We're all hurting,' he said.

At Garma I meet Marcia Langton – this woman who all those years ago had inspired me to go to university and helped me believe I could be a journalist. She is now Professor Langton, Chair of Indigenous Studies at Melbourne University. The old fire is still there, but she looks hollowed out, tired and drawn. How many times, she asks, do we have to put up with this – it is more a statement than a question. She is weary from a lifetime battling racism. Marcia is no firebrand radical separatist, she believes in communities being more accountable and argues for greater personal responsibility. She supported the Howard government's intervention in the Northern Territory. Marcia wants communities to become more empowered, to build more sustainable economies, to keep kids safe and in school. She has sought alliances with big business and government. But the treatment of Adam Goodes has reminded her that there is a primal, deep-seated racism here that she had hoped we had moved beyond.

In the coming days at Garma I will see old men in tears. 'We know your language,' one says, 'we go to your schools, we know your law, when will you learn ours?' Many of these people come from remote communities; places that some in governments – state and federal – have suggested should be shut down. These communities do present challenges; they are often small – sometimes a collection of just a few families – they are far from hospitals, shops and schools. Opportunities are limited. My own life has been a story of moving and embracing change; I can't deny that my horizons have broadened far beyond the small towns I was raised in. I have seen too how China has lifted hundreds of millions of people out of poverty by bringing them into larger urban centres. But the people at Garma remind me these places are their homes, their country – they fear being forced out. The old man with tears in his eyes, bangs the table and says, 'We will not be moved.'

At Garma I feel replenished. I feel the energy of my people. I am reconnected with those bonds of kinship, struggle and survival.

As I was asked what it feels like to be indigenous, I consider now what it is to be Australian. I have said how our anthem reminds us how hard it remains for us to rejoice. We can't be free when the weight of our history pins so many of us to the floor. Where is our wealth for toil? As a group we are the most impoverished people in this country.

As a people we have never truly figured in this nation's folklore; our stories don't fill the national imagination. Banjo Patterson, Henry Lawson – 'Clancy of the Overflow', 'The Man from Snowy River', and 'Joe Wilson and his Mates' don't speak to our experience. Ted Egan, the bush poet, came closer when he sang 'Poor Bugger Me Gurindji' in honour of Vincent Lingiari and the Wave Hill stockmen's strike that helped trigger the land rights movement. Vincent Lingiari receiving a handful of sand from then Prime Minister Gough Whitlam – recognising his right to land – that was us.

The sweeping plains and rugged mountain ranges may have fired Dorothea Mackellar's imagination, but as I have explained they were also places of death for our people. We were stricken by disease on those plains. We were herded over those mountains. After the coming of the settlers, this was the 'wide brown land' for us.

We find our peoplehood in the ancient nations of this land. For me it is Wiradjuri and Kamilaroi, for others Bandjalang or Luritja or Arrernte or Adnyamathanha or Yorta Yorta or any of the other hundreds of nations here before Europeans came.

Government policies have ranged from protection – preparing the passing of a race apparently destined for extinction – to segregation to assimilation to integration to self-determination. We fight still to be recognised in the

Australian Constitution; that same constitution that has allowed laws to take away children; invade our homes and violate our privacy.

In so many ways this country has told us we don't belong. If we hear it long enough we believe it. I have struggled to find a deeper allegiance to the myths and symbols of Australia. 'C'mon Aussie C'mon', zinc cream and crowds have never been a comfortable fit.

I am not alone. In 2015 Deborah Cheetham – indigenous performer and Associate Dean, Music, University of Melbourne – declined an invitation to sing the national anthem at the AFL Grand Final. It would have been the largest audience she had performed before. Yet, she says, she could not sing those words with sincerity.

Deborah was aware that she would have been singing in front of people who may well have been among those who booed Adam Goodes. Adam, himself, would not attend the Grand Final.

PART NINE

My son is stirring now in the backseat of our car. As he has slept I have driven in silence, gazing on the ebbs and flow of my land as I thought of the arc of my life and what lies ahead for him, for all of my children. I know sometimes they must find me distant, preoccupied. I have spent a lot of time away following the stories that have called me around the world. I am probably hard on them in many ways, I am like my father in this; I want them armed and ready for the world. It is harder for us; in the race for success we are starting from the back marker. They have had the benefit of good schools and privileges denied to me as a boy, but unlike many of their friends there is no inheritance of wealth; that was taken from us. What we have, we have made. The crippling poverty and death of our people hangs over their lives and mine. I have told them they live in a world where we have not made the rules so we need to be better at playing the game.

The winter of 2015 has shaken them as it has me. If Adam Goodes can be laid so low, then we are all at risk.

I have told them over and over that in this life we must cover up and never leave an opening for racism to strike us. If it does we must be ready to deliver a counterpunch. This is the lesson my father taught me when we strapped on the boxing gloves. The Adam Goodes booing debate, enraged me, sickened me, saddened me and made me feel at times helpless. Here was everything I had thought – hoped – we had left behind. It was repudiation of everything we say we value; everything we say has made us great. All of those words: tolerance, freedom, inclusion – I wondered now whether any of it was ever real. Certainly it has never felt real to us. For my children I hope it is a lesson learned – a reminder to harden themselves and make good on their talents; honour the legacy of their people.

This journey we have taken – my son and I – has been as much about me as him. I wanted to bring him out here to wrap him in his country. To show him where he is from and share the story of what happened to his people. But, it has stirred old memories for me. This year perhaps for the first time in a long time, I have needed to come back home – to my country: Wiradjuri country. I don't need Australia, I don't need to work here. I am comfortable in the world and the opportunities it offers. I could leave tomorrow and in so many ways not miss Australia. But I would miss my people; I would miss my parents. I would miss those connections that hold me against the loneliness of the world.

My son is hungry now and we stop at a roadside café. It strikes me how diverse our country is – how our faces have changed. There is an Islamic woman with her head covered; there is an African-American family, broad accents and girls with braided hair; there are Asian families. What in my childhood would have been exotic is now commonplace.

My mind returns to a story my father told me just the day before. He said he was in a similar café in a country town with my mother. He sat there as the waitress passed them by. Other customers came and went and still they weren't served. 'I don't know whether it was because we are Aboriginal,' he said. My father wants to believe deep down that Australia is better than its worst. Yet he knows racism remains just a harsh word, a disregarding look or a bigoted waitress away. My parents have spent a lifetime enduring this humiliation and now in a café in a country town he is reminded that it can still happen in 2015.

Here is the answer to that earlier question. Racism isn't killing the Australian dream. The Australian dream was founded on racism. From the first time a British flag was planted in this soil, the rules have been different for us. A convict could come in chains and die free, a rich man. But British law condemned us to a longer sentence.

This is my answer to that question posed that day in the ABC Radio studio: how does it feel to be indigenous? It feels hard – and we are tired. But, we have survived; we are nourished by our families and our culture, our story.

For all that has divided us we are here together in a land that has become home to us all. We can go nowhere else – and I have tried. There are white Australians who down the generations have become in their own way indigenous. They don't share our antiquity or our culture but they have made their own here and it has formed them. From wherever their ancestors' journeys began, these people are now from here; they can be from nowhere else.

It should be easier from where they stand to grasp how profound is our connection to country. I would like to think that with a sense of place comes a sense of history; an acceptance that what has happened here has happened to us all and that to turn from it or hide from it diminishes us.

We seek solutions. We like to imagine that there is one elusive answer. Governments make policy and we bear the consequences. Of course there is no 'indigenous community' – we are many and our issues myriad and diverse. But we know that we also share our fate and our connection runs deep. There are those Australians of all colours and creeds who stand with us. They have marched over bridges, stood in silent protest, wept with apology. They are perhaps the majority – I hope they are. But there are bigots, those who would divide us, and if they are smaller in number their words land on us with the force of history.

Australia has had many high points – those times when we thought we had finally begun to heal that wound on our soul. In the early years of settlement, Bennelong – an Eora man – set sail to Britain. In the 1820s Windradyne the Wiradjuri warrior marched into Parramatta to make peace. More than a hundred years later, Australia Day 1938, Aboriginal people stood in Sydney and declared a day of mourning. In 1967 Australians voted in overwhelming numbers, passing a referendum to count us among you – to recognise us as people. We have launched freedom rides to overturn segregation. We have pitched tents on the lawns of parliament to challenge your laws. We have won back our land. In 1992 – 204 years after settlement – the High Court struck down the fiction of *Terra nullius*. British law told Australia what we always knew: we were here.

Yet with each high point we seem to retreat. The apology was meant to atone for the Stolen Generations. Since that day the number of indigenous children removed from their families has increased by more than 400 per cent. Two decades after a royal inquiry into black deaths in custody the number of indigenous people locked up in Australia has grown 100-fold. We die younger, we go blind, babies are born deaf; our communities remain in crisis. An Aboriginal man – a sporting hero – can be driven from the game he loves.

In 2015 when the noise was at its loudest I tried to find a quiet way to talk of our experience. I looked to all that I had: words; just words, I sat in my room and I wrote:

I have wondered for days if I should say anything about Adam Goodes.

My inclination is to look for common ground, to be diplomatic. Some of the fault is with Adam. Maybe he's been unnecessarily provocative. Racism? Perhaps. Perhaps the crowds just don't like him.

Yes, I could make a case for all of that. But there are enough people making those arguments and all power to them.

Here's what I can do. I can tell you what it is like for us. I can tell you what Adam must be feeling, because I've felt it. Because every indigenous person I know has felt it.

It may not be what you want to hear. Australians are proud of their tolerance yet can be perplexed when challenged on race, their response often defensive.

I may be overly sensitive. I may see insult where none is intended. Maybe my position of relative success and privilege today should have healed deep scars of racism and the pain of growing up indigenous in Australia. The same could be said of Adam. And perhaps that is right.

But this is how Australia makes us feel. Estranged in the land of our ancestors, marooned by the tides of history on the fringes of one of the richest and demonstrably most peaceful, secure and cohesive nations on earth.

The 'wealth for toil' we praise in our anthem has remained out of our reach. Our position at the bottom of every socio-economic indicator tragically belies the Australian economic miracle.

'Australians all let us rejoice' can ring hollow to us. Ours is more troubled patriotism. Our allegiance to Australia, our pride in this country undercut by the dark realities of our existence.

Seeds of suspicion and mistrust are planted early in the indigenous child. Stories of suffering, humiliation and racism told at the feet of our parents and grandparents feed an identity that struggles to reconcile a pride in heritage with the forlorn realities of a life of defeat.

From childhood I often cringed against my race. To be Aboriginal was to be ashamed. Ashamed of our poverty. Ashamed of the second-hand clothes with the giveaway smell of mothballs and another boy's name on the shirt collar.

Ashamed of the way my mother and grandmother had to go to the Smith Family or Salvation Army for food vouchers. Ashamed of the onions and mince that made up too many meals.

We were ashamed of the bastardised wreckage of a

culture that we clung to. This wasn't the Dreamtime. This
was mangy dogs and broken glass.

Like the Goodes family, we moved constantly as my
father chased work. But wherever we went we found our
place always on the fringes. What semblance of pride
we carried too easily laid low by a mocking glance or a
schoolyard joke.

We were the blacks. So easily recognised not just by
the colour of our skin but by the whiff of desperation and
danger we cloaked ourselves in. What resentment we
harboured, we too often turned on ourselves, played out
in wild scrambling brawls from the playground to the
showgrounds that sent the same message: stay away from
the blacks.

There was humour and there was love and there was
survival. And as I grew older I pieced together the truth
that we didn't choose this. We are the detritus of the
brutality of the Australian frontier.

As Australia welcomed waves of migrants and built
a rich, diverse, tolerant society, we remained a reminder
of what was lost, what was taken, what was destroyed to
scaffold the building of this nation's prosperity.

We survived the 'smoothing of the dying pillow'
of extermination to end up on the bottom rung of the
ladder of assimilation. Too many of us remain there
still. Look to the statistics: the worst health, housing,

education, the lowest life expectancy, highest infant mortality. An indigenous youth has more chance of being locked up than educated.

If good fortune or good genes means you are among the lucky few to find an escape route then you face a choice: to 'go along to get along', mind your manners, count your blessings and hide in the comfort of the Australian dream; or to infuse your success with an indignation and a righteousness that will demand this country does not look away from its responsibilities and its history.

I found a path through education that led to journalism. A love of knowledge and an inquisitiveness that has shot me through with anger. A deeper understanding of history, of politics, of economics, leaving me resentful of our suffering.

I wrestle with that anger as the boy I was wrestled with his shame. I want to see the good in a society that defies the history of its treatment of my people.

It is the legacy of my grandfather who signed up to fight a war for a country that didn't recognise his humanity, let alone his citizenship. It is the lesson of the example of the lives of my mother and father, my uncles and aunties. Lives of decency and hard work and responsibility and rooted in our identity as indigenous Australians.

When I was sixteen I summoned the courage to speak to my class. As the only indigenous kid, the only Aboriginal person my schoolmates had met, I wanted to tell my family's story. My teacher was proud and encouraging. When class returned after lunch the words 'be kind to abos' were scrawled across the blackboard.

The rejection, the humiliation, cut me to the core.

This is the journey too of Adam Goodes. A man whose physical gifts have set him above and given him a platform available to so few and whose courage demands that he use it to speak to us all.

Events in recent years have sent Adam on a quest to understand the history of his people, to challenge stereotypes and perceptions. I have spoken to him about this. I recognise in him the same quest I see in myself. It is a conversation I have had with so many of my indigenous brothers and sisters.

This is rare air for anyone, let alone a footballer. He has faltered at times and the expression of his anger at our history and his pride in his identity has been challenging, if not divisive.

The events of 2013 when he called out a thirteen-year-old girl for a racial taunt opened a wound that has only deepened. To some the girl was unfairly vilified. Adam's war dance of this year challenged and scared some people. His talent, the way he plays the game, alienates others.

And now we have this, a crescendo of boos. The racial motivation of some giving succour to the variously defined hatred of others.

To Adam's ears, the ears of so many indigenous people, these boos are a howl of humiliation. A howl that echoes across two centuries of invasion, dispossession and suffering. Others can parse their words and look for other explanations, but we see race and only race. How can we see anything else when race is what we have clung to even as it has been used as a reason to reject us.

I found refuge outside Australia. My many years working in Asia, the Middle East, Europe and Africa liberated me. Here were the problems of other peoples and other lands. Here I was an observer freed from the shackles of my own country's history.

I still wonder if it would be easier to leave again.

But people – like Adam Goodes, other indigenous sportsmen and women who are standing with him, his non-indigenous teammates and rivals who support him, and my non-indigenous wife, my children and their friends of all colours and the people of goodwill who don't have the answers but want to keep asking questions of how we can all be better – maybe they all make it worth staying.

Now, the city is drawing near. I am a long way from the hills and rocks and trees of my land. Each time I leave it seems to get that bit harder. I wonder as I say goodbye to my mother and father, how many times I will see them again. Their lives have been hard but they have endured. They are past the age when most of our people die – they have buried so many of them. This time, for the first time, I sensed their mortality and it reminded me of my own. I hope I am here to hold my children's children. I hope I am around to tell them of their great-grandparents – my parents – and our lives on Australia's back roads.

In the coming days my son's life will fall back into the routines of school and friends. In the city we are all crowded together – all faces and names and languages and colours. We can so easily vanish – just a fraction of the population. The stories of history – Poison Waterholes Creek, Murdering Island – may fade from his mind as he thinks only of today, as all children do. But history shapes us even when we are not looking and there are many chapters still to be written.

I don't know if there will come a day when the past will be past. In me always will be the people of these pages – Wongamar and Windradyne and John Grant and Bill Grant – the storyteller. I will always sit by a river or stand on my land and hear the voices and see the faces of my people. My children and their children will be Wiradjuri people. My son will sit by Poison Waterholes Creek one day and tell the story to his son.

The traffic is growing thick. Next to me I can hear the thumping bass from a car stereo. In the distance the skyscrapers of the city are beckoning. The traffic light turns green.

My father has always told me: 'You will come home.' To a young boy with a head full of dreams of the world that seemed foolish. Why would I come back, when all I wanted was to get away? But I know what he means now. He wasn't talking about a place – he was talking my spirit. My spirit is home.

When I was back in Australia one summer after years overseas, I took one of my sons to the local swimming pool near my parents' house. I was reliving the great ritual of my childhood. As we walked down the burning concrete steps, another Aboriginal boy walked towards us. For a moment he locked eyes with my son – they stood just staring at each other. As we walked on my boy turned to me and asked: 'Why does he look like me?'

Why? Because this is where we are from.

My country: Australia.

Acknowledgments

I would like to thank my family for their love and a life time of stories. Thanks to my agent Tara Wynne (I know I am hopeless at returning calls and emails!). To everyone at HarperCollins, especially Catherine Milne for encouraging me and my editor Nicola Robinson for keeping me on track. My deep love to everyone at CNN who made me a reporter and showed me the world. To my people – you inspire me; I am so proud to be an Aboriginal man. Adam Goodes – stand tall. James Baldwin – forever and always my inspiration.

Selected Sources

Ahearne, J., *Michel de Certeau: Interpretation and its Other*, Polity Press, Cambridge, 1995.

Atwood, B. (ed.), *In the Age of Mabo: History, Aborigines and Australia*, Allen & Unwin, St Leonards, NSW, 1996.

Baldwin J., *The Evidence of Things Not Seen*, Henry Holt and Company, New York, 1995.

Baldwin, J., *The Fire Next Time*, Penguin Books, Harmondsworth, Middlesex, 1964.

Bennett, S., *White Politics and Black Australians*, Allen & Unwin, St Leonards, NSW, 1999.

Berndt, R.M., 'Wuradjeri Magic and "Clever Men"', *Oceania*, 1947, vol. 17, no. 4, pp. 327–365.

Blainey, G., *The Triumph of the Nomads: A History of Ancient Australia*, Macmillan, Melbourne, 1975.

Broome, R., *Aboriginal Australians: Black Responses to White Dominance, 1788–1980*, Allen & Unwin, St Leonards, NSW, 1982.

Cameron, K., 'Looking Back', unpublished, 2000.

Cathcart, M., *Manning Clark's History of Australia* (abridged), Melbourne University Press, Melbourne, 1993.

Chesterman, J., and Calligan, B., *Citizens Without Rights: Aborigines and Australian Citizenship*, Cambridge University Press, Melbourne, 1997.

Clayton, I., 'Warengesda [sic] births deaths and marriages', Canberra, AIATSIS, PMS 4577, 1988.

Coates, T., *Between the World and Me*, Text Publishing Company, Melbourne, 2015.

Cowlishaw, G., *Rednecks, Eggheads and Blackfellas: A Study of Racial Power and Intimacy in Australia*, Allen & Unwin, St Leonards, NSW, 1999.

Fink, R., 'The Caste Barrier: An Obstacle to the Assimilation of part-Aborigines in the North West of New South Wales', *Oceania*, 1957, vol. 28, no. 2, pp. 100–110.

Genovese, E.D., *Roll, Jordan, Roll: The World the Slaves Made*, Vintage Books, New York, 1976.

Gilbert, K.J., *Because a White Man'll Never Do It*, HarperCollins, Sydney, NSW, 2013. (first pub. 1973)

Goodall, H., *Invasion to Embassy: Land in Aboriginal Politics in New South Wales, 1770–1972*, Allen & Unwin, St Leonards, NSW, 1996.

Grant, C., *The Cec Grant/Wongamar Story*, The Teachers' Collection, Wagga Wagga, NSW, 1996.

Grant, J., *Providence: The Life and Times of John Grant (1792–1866)*, J. Grant, Orange, NSW, 1994.

Grant, S., *The Tears of Strangers*, HarperCollins, Sydney, NSW, 2002.

Gribble, Rev. J.B., 'Collected Papers 1873–1905', AIATSIS, MS 1514, 1982.

Harare, Y.N., *Sapiens: A Brief History of Humankind*, Harvill Secker, London, 2014.

Hughes, R., *The Fatal Shore: A History of the Transportation of Convicts to Australia 1787–1868*, Pan Books in association with Collins, London, 1988.

Keed, R., *Memories of Bulgandramine Mission*, R. Keed, Peak Hill, NSW, 1985.

Langton, M., '"Well, I heard it on the radio and I saw it on the television": An essay for the Australian Film Commission on the politics and aesthetics of film making by and about Aboriginal people and things', Australian Film Commission, North Sydney, NSW, 1993.

McGregor, A., *Cathy Freeman: A Journey Just Begun*, Random House Australia, Milsons Point, NSW, 1998.

Manne, R.M., *In Denial: The Stolen Generations and the Right*, Schwartz Publishing, Melbourne, 2001.

Marable, M., *Malcolm X: A Life of Reinvention*, Penguin Books, London, 2012.

Markus, A., *Race: John Howard and the Remaking of Australia*, Allen & Unwin, Crows Nest, NSW, 2001.

Moore, L., and Williams, S., *The True Story of Jimmy Governor*, Allen & Unwin, Crows Nest, NSW, 2001.

Pearson, M., 'Bathurst Plains and Beyond: European Colonisation and Aboriginal Resistance', *Aboriginal History*, 1984, vol. 8, no. 1, pp. 63–79.

Pearson, N., 'White Guilt, Victimhood and the Quest for a Radical Centre', *Griffith Review* 16, ABC Books, Sydney, 2007.

Price, S., '"They're Still Killing Us": Black Deaths in Custody', *Redflag*, January 2015.

Read, P., 'A History of the Wiradjuri People of NSW, 1883–1969', Thesis (Ph.D.), Australian National University, Canberra, AIATSIS, ms 1850, 1983.

Reynolds, H., *Aboriginal Sovereignty: Reflections on Race, State and Nation*, Allen & Unwin, St Leonards, NSW, 1996.

Reynolds, H. (ed.), *Dispossession: Black Australia and White Invaders*, Allen & Unwin, Sydney, 1989.

Rowley, C.D., *Outcasts in White Australia*, ANU Press, Canberra, 1971.

Rowley, C.D., *The Destruction of Aboriginal Society*, Penguin Books Australia, Ringwood, Vic, 1972.

Salisbury T., and Gresser, P.J., *Windradyne of the Wiradjuri: Martial Law at Bathurst in 1824*, Wentworth Books, Sydney, 1971.

Scott, R., and Heiss, A. (eds.), *The Intervention: an Anthology*, Concerned Australians, 2015.

Stanner, W.E.H., *After the Dreaming*, ABC Enterprises, Crows Nest, NSW, 1991.

Stanner, W.E.H., 'The History of Indifference Thus Begins', *Aboriginal History*, 1977, vol. 1, no. 1, pp. 3–26.

Suttor, W.H., *Australian Stories Retold, and, Sketches of Country Life*, Glyndwr Whalan, Bathurst, NSW, 1887.

Walker, C., *Buried Country: The Story of Aboriginal Country Music*, Pluto Press, Sydney, 2000.